AS I SEE
NOW

As I See Now
Published by RBG Books LLC
www.RBGbookstore.com

Copyright © 2023 Bonny Grosz

All rights reserved. No part of this book may be reproduced in any form or by any electronic or mechanical means, including photocopying, recording, or by any information storage and retrieval systems, without permission in writing from the publisher except by reviewers, who may quote brief passages in a review.

Library of Congress Control Number: 202392230
ISBN 978-1-7377380-6-0 (Hardcover)
ISBN 978-1-7377380-4-6 (Paperback)
ISBN 978-1-7377380-5-3 (Digital Edition)

Book design and typography by Ismail Ogunbiyi and Janice Levie.
Cover design by Cheakina.

Printed in the United States of America

To the reader:
Throughout this book's "Transmissions" section, the editor's comments are italicized and preceded by the heading "From the Transcriber." Rabbi Hayyim's comments, editorial, and other remarks are bracketed (not italicized).

AS I SEE NOW

---◆---

The Wisdom,
Insights and Recollections
of Hayyim Vital

---◆---

Rabbi Bonny Grosz
Transcriber and Editor

RBG Books LLC

This book is dedicated to the Wisdom and the Light that true teachers bring into our world and to the students who carry on the work in the names of those teachers for the good of all.

CONTENTS

From Rabbi Vital to the Transcriber iii

INTRODUCTION v

From the Transcriber vii
Rabbi Vital's Disclaimer x
How to Read This Book xi

THE TRANSMISSIONS 1

Early Encounters 3
Truth, Wisdom, and Knowledge 9
Readiness 12
Repackaging 21
Unification with the Divine 22
Paths to Unification 27
More About Truth, Wisdom, and Knowledge 35
Redemption 39
Joy 53
Spiritual Technologies 67
Shifting Perspectives and Perceptions 73
Mystical Authenticity 105
Repairing the World 113
Holy Time and Space: The Sabbath 122
To Be of This World 126
Reincarnation 149
More About Redemption 164
The Soul Root and the Oversoul 167
Inspiration and Impermanence 179

    The Secret of Life 181
    Bring It All Together 184
    Knowing 186
    Bound by Fear 190
    Suffering and Restriction 194
    The Book of Visions 196
    The Wonder and Marvel of Creation 202
    Messages 205
    Consequence 209
    On Women 216
    The Truth of Self 219

APPENDIX 221
    Safed and Rabbinic Biographies 223
    Rabbi Hayyim Vital 226
    The Maggid of Rabbi Yosef Karo 232
    Shabbatai Tzvi 234
    Four Who Entered the Garden 236
    The Kabbalistic Tree of Life 238

ACKNOWLEDGMENTS 240

REFERENCES 242

ABOUT THE TRANSCRIBER 245

FROM RABBI VITAL TO THE TRANSCRIBER

This is the time, and you are committed. Together, we will bring life to subjects of the most esoteric nature. We will record a personal and practical account of a time, place, and people that will not be geared toward scholars, although it comes from a scholarly background. Our work is to be directed to a larger, more universal audience who may benefit from any wisdom I may be blessed to pass on to them.

So far, what has been written by others mostly reconstructs the recollections and legends of those who were either present with or who came soon after me. As with all recollections, they have evolved and been embellished through time and the telling. Some are true, some are based on Truth, some are wishful narratives, and some are completely misinformed.

Here, you will witness some of my views of what came to pass in my day and with me.

— Rabbi Hayyim ben Yosef Vital
(Rabbi Bonny Grosz, Transcriber, and Editor)
June 10, 2019

INTRODUCTION

FROM THE TRANSCRIBER

Sometimes, a still, small voice calls upon us to take on a task. We may not hear the call at first, but the voice persists until we are ready to receive its message. For some, readiness only comes when the voice grows louder, and then a celestial two-by-four gets our attention.

Such was my experience in 2006 as I prepared a thesis for my rabbinical ordination.[1] While immersed in a pile of publications about sixteenth-century Safed, the Kabbalists, their texts, and their practices, I heard Rabbi Hayyim Vital's slow, steady voice clearly tell me that I was to write his story. He was very bold, concise, and declarative: in no uncertain terms, I was to correct and clarify what he had written during his time on Earth. This new account would be developed from his current perspective, which was no longer bound by the restrictions of his physical existence.

So much demanded my attention at that time that I shuddered when I thought of an additional massive undertaking, never mind that the request was coming from a sixteenth-century luminary. Still, when I attempted to regain my composure and sat looking out my window, R. Hayyim's voice grew louder, jarring me from disbelief to confusion, from confusion to awe, and from awe to acceptance. I felt my heart soften with humility for having been chosen for such a holy endeavor, and I knew I was meant to honor his request.

I did not hear from R. Hayyim again until 2014. I was finally unencumbered by some of my previous obligations and on a road

---

[1] The topic of the thesis was Cheshbon HaNefesh (An Accounting of the Soul).

trip to explore parts of the United States I had never visited. On my first day out, R. Hayyim approached me at a small café in the middle of West Virginia. I was taken aback but calmly grabbed a napkin and started recording his words, careful not to acknowledge his presence in front of the other patrons.

He continued to make himself known to me at the oddest times (usually when I was dining in a restaurant or driving), and he spoke with varying degrees of continuity and focus (at once directing me to read background material and then interrupting with tales of his life and contemporaries). He was quick to remind me that those who documented his life and times did not always understand the truth. How could they? Some were not in his inner circle, and others were not of his time. His reminders worked their way into many of our conversations, as did his promise of "more to come."

I'd sensed his urgency and insistence as far back as 2006, but never so much as when he contacted me again in 2019 while I was living in Cairo. He visited me daily at the Sufi Café, where I spent untold hours each day recording his words. In 2020, we continued our work at the edge of the desert outside of Las Vegas, Nevada. Between 2019 and 2020, we completed most of the book's text in "The Transmissions" section. "The Transmissions" contains many layers, with hints and clues intended to bring deeper meaning and profound lessons to the larger text of life.

I finally edited his transmissions during the second half of 2022 and the beginning of 2023, having been led to one who was sent to assist me in completing this work.

═══◆═══

INTRODUCTION

As I See Now presents a variety of truths through messages that realign historical facts and provide insight into R. Hayyim's psyche from a higher perspective than what we can know within the confines of life while we are living it. The book is for anyone interested in R. Hayyim's fascinating, pivotal period in history, and especially his spiritual teachings, which remind us of our purpose on Earth and what we are here to learn. His words are relevant to all, even those who never heard of him.

What I discovered triggered a deeper understanding of life and of "self" (based on my place in the world today). I sincerely hope that you, too, connect with the heart of its writer, R. Hayyim Vital, and that his words become as much a blessing to you as they are to me.

— Rabbi Bonny Grosz
Transcriber and Editor
February 2023

RABBI VITAL'S DISCLAIMER

This volume is not an academic endeavor. There is already enough written from an intellectual perspective about me and my writings. I thought at first my purpose was to make revisions and corrections to theories and practices I had in my original works, but then I found myself drawn to speak of things closer to my heart that would be more helpful to others. In the process, I found new insights about myself and the messages that pertain to the world throughout history. Perhaps in the future, I shall address the corrections to my works and the perceptions that have followed me historically. As for academics? Let them understand my writings better, having learned more about me and how my writings came to be.

— Rabbi Hayyim ben Yosef Vital
(Rabbi Bonny Grosz, Transcriber, and Editor)
December 12, 2019

HOW TO READ THIS BOOK

Before beginning "The Transmissions," you may want to familiarize yourself with R. Hayyim's life and times by referring to the Appendix. While reading "The Transmissions," be aware of the following:

- When R. Hayyim seems to be speaking to the Transcriber, he is almost always also speaking to you, the reader.

- R. Hayyim sometimes uses "we" when referring to his sixteenth-century contemporaries. He also uses "we" when referring to all humanity and, at times, the Oversoul. (See "Spiritual Technology" in "The Transmissions.")

- "The Transmissions" section is edited to clarify what might otherwise be wordy and awkward to the modern ear. [Bracketed] text indicates what Hayyim sought to have clarified and to present supplemental information.

- R. Hayyim's words appear in standard font. The Transcriber's words are italicized and preceded by "From the Transcriber."

- Some transmissions quote or cite passages from R. Hayyim's and others' works. Such instances indicate the Transcriber's corroboration of the words with the many resources that informed R. Hayyim's life.

THE TRANSMISSIONS

EARLY ENCOUNTERS

July 7, 2014

From the Transcriber

R. Hayyim seems to enjoy our conversations and often initiates them when I am dining out. He first approached me unexpectedly in Berkeley Springs, West Virginia, while I was having lunch at a cute little café in the middle of town. He quickly became my companion at most meals, even though I always requested a table for one. Early on, he introduced me to new topics to explore on the internet. Occasionally, he interjected comments on what I was reading about him. "That's not right, you know," he would say, or "What do you think about that?" Mostly, he would say, "Keep reading, keep reading." He knew the questions my mind was creating and answered each question as it came up.

While I was reading his works, he commented, "I know that sounds quite stringent to you, but it was the times, you know," and "I want to tell you what I now know from my new perspective." As he explained:

> 'No matter how creative the mind, it can only have so much range of function in the Earth realm. Thoughts, intellect, and, yes, even wisdom are subject to the confines in which it is encased. And so, it is necessary (for me) to now tell you from a

new perspective. Yes, in a way, I am editing my work from more than four centuries ago. There is new material that I wish to put forth and material I wish to correct. Together, we will decide what form this will take.'

Even now, as I read some of the background material, I hear him tell me that everything may not be relevant, but not to worry — just keep reading.

August 13, 2014
―――――――――――――――――――――――――

It wasn't always the way they said it was. I had my own revelations, or *Bat Kol* [Divine voice] — although I allowed myself to be called the disciple of this one or that one. I did not understand that "the power" had been given to me directly. I did not know I stood apart as an individual and that all I needed was within me. The vastness of what was given to me I knew intellectually but did not know in my heart. [The structure of the times and our society contributed to my misperceptions.] I always put the other's work above mine and what was given to me directly. I tried to make it fit into the pattern of how the power was given to others. As I told you, it was the times and the way things had to be for me to be accepted. Strange how that works, isn't it?

When you look everywhere, your horizon is so expanded that you easily miss that which is close to you. We are close now. We are always close, and yet you only sometimes know this.

═══◆═══

It is challenging to step outside of prescribed patterns, even when they seem innovative. You, too, have tried to work from the "inside" but found it too difficult. You have wanted to, but it has been impossible. And so, before we continued with this work, you needed to understand "bigness," permitting and even accepting your bigness. Because of the times and my situation, I could do this to a greater degree than you. Your persona and my persona have much in common. You are no doubt surprised [about this]. So, it is to this kindred spirit that I speak.

August 19, 2014

From the Transcriber

A potential altercation between me and a server in a restaurant reminded me of the extent to which our choice of words and attitudes determine a situation's resolution. The incident presented me with the opportunity to relax my expectations and feel compassion for another when I took a moment to follow my inner knowing rather than my reactive self-consciousness. I was amused and pleased to feel the approval of my teachers, including R. Hayyim.

———◆———

What you describe is the only way to obtain peace. Do you see this now? We can conquer the issues you are addressing by having these meetings and dealing with life as it happens. Having a friend who gives perspective is nice, and I can be that friend.

Well, yes, to answer the question that I hear you asking in your mind: Am I the soul of Hayyim Vital, though I do not sound like him exactly? There is more of me coming forth at the moment than just him [that particular aspect of his soul]. Now, I seem more familiar to you — yes? I will explain.[2]

———✦———

From the Transcriber
You seem larger and yet more subtle than Hayyim's personality.

———✦———

Yes, when one focuses on the personality aspect of a soul, it seems more intense in a three-dimensional way. Please know I am [we are] available to you from this point on during your life journey. ["We" refers to the currently unembodied who already or may communicate with you.] Some sources of communication come and go according to the circumstances and stages of a lifetime. Sources may vary due to human choices, changed trajectories, and adjustments to original plans concerning guides and other assistance to the human. Yes, you know this, but many others do not, and so I say it for them and to remind you. We are familiar with one another. I have inhabited the bodies of many whom you have known over time.

---

[2] Years later, it was revealed to me that the voice speaking here was the Oversoul, which included but was not exclusively Hayyim's as explained in the chapter, "The Root Soul and the Oversoul."

TRUTH, WISDOM, AND KNOWLEDGE

June 2, 2019

A simple idea can potentially unlock wisdom, but not when its explanation is so complex that few can find meaning in it — including the very folks for whom the thought is intended.

It is the obligation of the spiritually evolved to remind the world that True Wisdom is always simple. The essence of Wisdom is always simple: it is always easy to comprehend and integrate for those who have arrived at a spiritual level to do so. Still, those less evolved spiritually will often "take the ball and run with it," as you say, and they will run so far with it that the Wisdom is no longer comprehensible, rendering it useless.

True Wisdom is transmitted in a variety of fashions, few of which require words. The longer the teaching, or the greater the number of words used to convey the teaching, the less likely the veracity. It began like this, with an abundance of words in my group of peers, but, as with so many others throughout human history, what seemed like evolution was actually the devolution of Knowledge. And today, I tell you that with time and distance, such as they are, comes reconsideration of the ideas and perspectives of what some accepted and developed as Truth in the confines of the third dimension. The truth about Truth is that it never has to be developed. And Truth is always simple. Truth simply IS.

The path to Truth is not always simple for most. Upon reaching [or they have reached] the endpoint, most mistake the complexities of their journey with the essence of Truth. They layer the Ultimate [Truth] with the twists and turns they encounter on their own path to that Truth. The way need not be so complex, but since many complicate everything in their lives, why should the way to Truth and the One [Source] be different? Finding one's way is not a matter of intelligence; it is a method of working out the aspects and lessons of the soul while embodied.

I was always so anxious to do things right that I often missed the point of life. I was too often distracted by my own ego and what I thought was the rightness of things that I did not allow for the infinite possibilities that life presents us with *on the path* and not what we believed to be the endpoint.

In life, I was drawn to the intellectually complex and the brilliance of the [intellectual and spiritual] stars around me, but somewhere inside, I knew the real path was a simple, straight line. I was attracted more to the Light that was shining from the human stars who knew of the simplicity to a greater degree than I was attracted to the Light within me. This has been the way for many throughout human existence, with little change.

Consciousness and awareness of the inner Light are accessible to many more today, but most doubt their ability to access it when they are blinded by those who proclaim to have found and know the way. The more complex the way of the teaching and the louder they speak of the Light, the more you should know that theirs is not your way. Some think of themselves as luminaries by whose Light others should be guided. Yet the genuine, authentic leaders on the path are luminaries who give Light without personally recognizing their own luminescence. Their inner Light provides inspiration and vision of what they have found within themselves — and they demonstrate this by how they live rather than by the methods they teach or the words they speak.

READINESS

June 6, 2019

I was taught too much at an early age when I did not have the life experience to absorb and handle all the information [appropriately]. You see, this difficulty occurs when elders perceive talent, intellect, or potential greatness in young ones. They are desperate to pass on what they know — intuitive and acquired knowledge alike — and forget that the young human may not be mature enough to integrate the information in a safe and balanced way. And so, it was with me. I was pushed too far, too fast, and never quite gained the necessary balance and stability in life. I would like you to know that this was all done with great love for me. The essential elements of life balance are absent when cerebral pursuits take over.

As you know, all may seem well with someone who keeps up appearances enough so that an imbalance goes unnoticed by the person and others. Still, the imbalance does begin to manifest in subtle and not-so-subtle ways. Sometimes, the person is labeled difficult, moody, or told they do not fit in. Some can fool even those who are close to them. Sadly, veiling the imbalance can increase it and lead to one's inability to manage life or even a total breakdown.

Those who hold and teach the Knowledge are gifted with it, but not as often are they also gifted with the wisdom and sensibility to see an imbalance within their students. Without the life experience and emotional maturity to integrate knowledge, there is a greater possibility of a break in the human psyche. Depending on the circumstances of one's life, a break may come sooner, or it may come later. There is no telling when or if a breakdown might occur, but there is what you call "wear and tear" along the way.

To tell the truth, only the most extraordinary humans can balance advanced esoteric knowledge with their seemingly ordinary day-to-day existence. Great, wise, and learned rabbis saw a receptacle for their teachings in me. But they did not assess my readiness to bear [sustain and support] the truths and knowledge they passed on. I had to hold much of the teaching somewhere inside me and try to retrieve it later. Sometimes, the teaching did not seem to penetrate my brain or being at all, and sometimes it did enter me. Still, I was unable to integrate the knowledge successfully. The teachings were more than a child or young man could handle or hold.

It is important — no, essential — that one does not ascend too quickly in any field. When inadequately prepared, it is possible to ascend for moments but not as a practice or way of life. Would one go up in a rocket without the proper training or gear in your world?

The momentary Unification [with Source] that humans sometimes experience may hasten their awakening by hinting at what is possible. The person can then choose to follow the pursuit of Unification or not.³ One usually works within the parameters of one's time and place but occasionally stretches beyond those parameters. The paths to Unification are many, and I have to say [they are] rarely the ones I put forth in my works and the works I recorded on behalf of others. We [myself and my contemporaries] often had a very narrow view of things when we did our work [despite the fact our work was cosmically expansive]. Of course, we did not think so then. But that is for another time.

I emphasize the need to have reached an appropriate level of maturity before inundating and over-educating a person, regardless of age. Outreach and teaching by a person who is not emotionally ready may very well be twisted and cause real damage to the student and *the world*. [I am saying that the one who learns unprepared and then teaches unprepared can cause this situation.] We never know who listens when we teach, so we must be vigilant about our thoughts and words and who receives them. Naturally, we do not have precise knowledge of everyone's maturity, and this is where discernment enters the picture. If we have learned inappropriate knowledge at an inappropriate time, we will unlikely recognize the need [or capacity for] appropriate and useful discernment. For some, discernment is quite intuitive. Others require more focus and training to hone their skills.

You might wonder about the word "inappropriate." What seems inappropriate is not really, since all is part of the learning process in all individuals' lives and the world in which they find

---

³ *Yichud* (Unification) refers to drawing closer to God, The Source of All Creation, achieved by the various methods and spiritual technologies used throughout human history. *Yichud* can also mean a unification with the spirit of another, but in almost every reference made in this text, it refers to Unification with Source.

themselves. Nevertheless, individuals can choose to take learning in a different direction.

I excelled at teaching, prayer, and study but suffered greatly from managing everyday life. I did not recover from the overload of the "high" [elevated] knowledge I received too soon. It affected my relationships and every aspect of my daily life. I did not outwardly shine as brightly as some in my circle, but we each had a role to play. I played mine well, but I will discuss this in another context.

For now, this is enough on the topic.

June 13, 2019

From the Transcriber

Some accounts say that R. Hayyim was not immediately drawn to the newly arrived Rabbi Isaac Luria upon the passing of his teacher, Rabbi Moshe Cordovero (the RaMaK). But shortly thereafter, R. Hayyim was not only drawn to HaAri but quickly became his chief disciple. We learn in Vital's own Book of Visions that the main purpose of Luria's move to Safed was to teach Hayyim Vital.

Having become acquainted somewhat with R. Hayyim's nature through his transmissions to me, I would say that what seemed like reluctance to others was actually out of respect or deference to his recently deceased teacher. He did not want to betray his loyalty to his former teacher. Legend has it that the RaMaK appeared to him in a dream a few months after his passing. When R. Hayyim adjured him to tell him the truth — whether they should study Kabbalah according to his system or according to HaAri's in the Heavenly Academy[4] — *his former teacher replied,*

> *'Both approaches are true. However, my approach is the simple one, suitable for beginners in the wisdom of Kabbalah, whereas the teachings of your teacher [HaAri] are deeper and are the primary approach. I, too, in the Heavenly Academy, now study only according to the approach of your present master.'*[5]

———◆———

This story is interesting because the information was passed on from *Olam Habah*.[6] This tradition is long honored in our circle. What we see from the new perspective, from *Olam Habah*, is usually quite clear. We reach levels of clarity incrementally as the soul progresses on its journey through various realms. And so, what is extremely complex in the Earth realm becomes much clearer and simpler the further away we travel from it [as we see

---

[4] "In rabbinic tradition, a heavenly body of scholars. Post-mishnaic (talmudic and midrashic) literature speaks of an Academy on High, for which two terms are used: *'Yeshivah shel Ma'lah'* ('Academy on High') and *'Metivta de-Raki'a'* ('Academy of the Sky'). It is clear from *Bava Mezia 86a* that the two terms are identical. Generally speaking, the Academy on High has the same features as an earthly academy. Scholars continue their studies and debates there; therefore the death of a sage is expressed as a summons to the Academy on High (BM 86a)."
See Harry Freedman, "Academy on High," *Jewish Virtual Library*, accessed December 29, 2022, https://www.jewishvirtuallibrary.org/academy-on-high.
[5] Hayyim Vital, *The Book of Visions*, in *The Classics of Western Spirituality, A Library of the Great Spiritual Masters*, Trans. Morris M. Faierstein, Mahwah: Paulist Press, 1999, 2:17, p. 90.
[6] *Olam Habah* (The World to Come). This term refers to a state of being that exists (after physical death) as a reward for right actions of a person during their lifetime. With right action during the physical lifetime, one merits a place in the World to Come – *Olam Habah*.

it from a higher perspective]. The distractions and density of the material world no longer impede us from seeing clearly. Also, as with any pursuit in the physical world, what we see may become clearer with time and familiarity [and distance from them].

This may seem confusing since I tell you in other segments of this transmission that all is much simpler than we originally proposed. I do not mean just simpler for those of us who are unrestricted by physical bodies on Earth, but also less complicated in your realm. It is as though a dense cloud exists between your world and the clarity of our perspective. Some of you can permeate this cloud to a degree when you are ready to see clearly. Greater understanding is achieved with experience and perspective, allowing for the more complex and esoteric teachings to be easily pursued and digested. And so, I make my point about weighty and complex knowledge taught to those who are not yet prepared. It is not that they cannot comprehend it intellectually but that some teachings do not belong solely to the intellect.

If the purpose of the knowledge is an increased [and perceived] unity with the Creator, then isolated intellectual comprehension is insufficient. Information needs to be processed and integrated within a human being who has the maturity to bear witness and experience the union deeply with the soul, not only the mind. These two, the soul and the mind, generally operate in isolation from one another in most people, as one can often not support the experience of the other. Speaking from the perspective of the Heavenly Academy, I tell you that the two are unified with the capacity to grasp and support all that comes their way. Once again, this is my point about the importance of maturity and life experience before learning the Torah's inner workings and other esoteric teachings. There are also things I can neither tell you nor put into this work because those who are in physical form, with all its limitations, need to be ready to grasp the information — and they are not.

Safed's intellectual and spiritual "altitudes" were indeed rather lofty, especially when students and devotees came together to learn from the individuals who had reached great heights on their own. There was no limit to the heights we could achieve together with our combined spirits and abilities. The [almost] unlimited level of unification with the Divine could only be reached with Divine Inspiration. Let us now call it a Divine Invitation. The ink on the "invitation" contains the knowledge and secrets necessary for Unification.

The spiritual levels that could be reached with previously known methodologies and the practice of moral intellect were limited because of operating systems of man's design. [Anything man creates is limited in scope.] In the early times, these Divine Invitations were only delivered to a carefully chosen few and were accepted by even fewer. Over time, as invitations became more selective and exclusive, man succumbed to the ruling of the human intellect as opposed to Divine Inspiration or Invitation. Hence, this limited just how "high" one could soar in the state of ascension.

When we can subsume the intellect, there is room to join with the One, the Source of All Creation. Intellectually, there is no limit to the number of ways man can create systems for this, but the union neither takes place in the mind nor requires intellect! The mind cannot even articulate the experience aptly in human language after the union occurs. The systems developed to aid humans and direct them toward the state of the union are feeble and too corrupt to accomplish their intended purpose. It may seem confusing to you that the mind attempts to create pathways to something it can neither experience nor articulate. This is the way of the human experience in many arenas, and it is indeed confusing.

The above illustrates the main point of clarifying and simplifying my work from the late 1500s to the early 1600s. I do not discredit what we did, for at the time we had to work with what we knew. That is the best any man can do — operate with all that is available to him. The state of being we taught about and strove to activate is much easier to achieve than we proposed.

———◆———

From the Transcriber

Rabbi Hayyim remarked that the works of earlier Kabbalists, from the time after the RaMBaN [Nachmanides (1195–1270)] until HaAri, were built on moral intellect. In contrast, the teachings of his master, HaAri, were revelations received by HaAri through Ruach HaKodesh [Divine inspiration].[7]

---

[7] See Moshe Miller, "Rabbi Chaim Vital," *Chabad.org: Kabbalah Online*, accessed August 27, 2022, https://www.chabad.org/kabbalah/article_cdo/aid/380648/jewish/Rabbi-Chaim-Vital.htm.

REPACKAGING

June 15, 2019

It is time for repackaging. That is the term we can use — repackaging. You have sat doing research for an afternoon and came upon many enlightening historical and theological bits of information that sparked this thought in me. Yes, each age comes to its own conclusions, and few are new. They are almost all merely the repackaging of previous thoughts and revelations. It has been essential in most times, even in this one, that revelatory information reaches only those who are ready for it and who will not use it wrongly. Yes, you read that Shabbatai Tzvi[8] misused HaAri's work. This is what can and did happen and is the main reason for the secrecy surrounding the revealed Truths. In the wrong hands, the information would be misinterpreted and wrongly used, invalidating its [divinity and holy nature] and causing [intended and unintended] collateral damage.

---

[8] See "Shabbatai Tzvi" in the Appendix.

UNIFICATION WITH THE DIVINE

June 15, 2019

From the Transcriber
If you were to sum up the purpose of our work together, what would you say is its essence?

---◆---

You have understood the essence of my message already. It is to let people know where the secret — or that which seems to elude them and thereby seems like a secret — lies in achieving union with the Divine and thereby reaching at least half of their soul mission on Earth. We [well, not me at this moment] commit to life on the planet for specific purposes. There are both general and more detailed reasons for how the development of each cloaked human soul progresses. Not one of these things I mention warrants further explanation [although while in the Earthly life, you may think so]. And so we will work on that today, piece by piece, and I will attempt to explain it as seamlessly and simply as possible.

When we slide into the complexities of ideas and life, we lose sight of the original truth of the matter and others' intentions. Often, that is the underlying purpose of the complex methodologies created by the intelligentsia — to lose people's attention, thereby excluding the masses from the start, or to lose as many as possible along the way. Now, though, it is time to address my original statement of today's writing.

Two main reasons for incarnating on the Earth are 1) to experience the duality of creation, that is, the separation from the Divine energy of the Creator, thereby having to figure out how to act and grow with other humans in a way that cannot be experienced at the soul level, and; 2) to experience that duality by achieving Union with the Divine while in the human state, thereby maintaining the conscious connection between the created and its Source.

What is expected of us? What is expected of us is to maintain a tie with the Creator while operating in what appears to be a non-divine system. We are to fully participate in earthly life while recognizing and actively maintaining that Divine connection. In most regards, the experience is highly individual and individualized; it is rarely the same for any two people. Some may walk similar paths for a while, and their mission or approach may appear the same — and maybe, but only for a moment. We all have "contracts" to assist one another with our human and Divine connections and what we are here to learn.

As I dictated the above statement, with almost every word, I had to battle the inclination to elaborate, to pull in previous textual sources and references, and to make the whole business considerably more detailed than necessary. It is my hope you have the ability to avoid this pitfall of over-elaboration and confounding complexity.

Throughout history, once something has been discovered, there are those, though well-meaning, who will paper over the original and natural walls of the house [of Truth] with their version of what will make it all more beautiful and meaningful [to them]. The wallpapering usually continues until the teaching is no longer recognizable as the original or even what the revisionists set out to create. As it continues, the teaching is adjusted to each individual's taste and what works for them — what they and possibly no others will be able to live with or understand how anyone else cannot. The nakedness of the natural beauty and original Truth is covered and lost as only the One, the Builder, can remember it. And now, humans have become so involved with decorating that any memory of the original plan has faded.

There is no such thing as faith, only the remembering of Source.

June 20, 2019

You have done even more research now and are becoming more familiar with the teachers and works of my time, enough so that you are upset to see what you thought was my work attributed to another. Your role is to be a dispassionate observer in this matter so that the work is as close to pure as possible. This is a lesson all who study this topic (and most topics) must learn, so we shall now make it "a teaching." We must be sufficiently passionate about our aspirations to realize them but not so passionate that we lose our way through the overexpression of ego.

Any idea may potentially present a direction we had not previously considered. When we align too strongly with an idea, method, or process to the exclusion of others, we know the ego has become passionate and that we have lost our way. I believe you say, "Keep your eye on the prize." That prize is where you are headed, and if you align yourself only with your method of getting to the prize, you will not just slow yourself down but probably derail yourself altogether.

I sense that you deeply connect this message to your present-day world politics. Everything I tell you applies to your present world, and it all needs to be urgently relayed *at this time in your history*. The situation was not as all-consuming when I first called upon you, and the immediacy was not as apparent as it is now. Now there is a panic of many sorts, and it is even more critical to educate the population about ways going forward that will manifest the best possible world. If people cannot take to the principles of behavior we teach, they cannot create a better situation for themselves or the world. This eternal truth is often forgotten. It is endlessly learned and forgotten and then learned and forgotten once more. It is time to be learned again and, this time, not forgotten.

———◆———

Another topic I want to speak to you about is the dissemination of content. You have read that HaAri's teachings were written down only by me. Several of his students wanted to create their own groups after his passing, setting themselves up as teachers. Their writings were mainly for their own teaching and promotion, and after HaAri's life/body was no longer on this Earth, others recalled and mostly took down his words for their own use, despite his wishes. HaAri desired to pass the information orally from the teacher to the chosen student. He did not want his words or works recorded for posterity because he knew their power and complexity would be misconstrued, misused, and abused by people for personal and self-serving reasons. Because of their complexity, the inner secrets of the works were simultaneously hidden and visible in plain sight.

Some saw the complexity of his ideas and walked away or perhaps thought of someone they knew who might be capable of further explanation. But if they genuinely did not understand, they were not meant to. Then there were those who believed that they alone understood, some out of the need to be "in the know," some because they felt they understood everything, and some because of the shame that not understanding something would bring them. All of this, as you can see, is ego-based. The ego of one who desires to "crack the code" leads them to others of ego, who also were not meant to decipher the meaning. Again, when the ego is involved, everybody loses.

It was important for me to preserve HaAri's words by transcribing them, whether anyone would read them or not. I did not think the brilliant life's work of my beloved teacher should be lost to humankind and history, so I transcribed my notes of his teachings and put them out into the world — or rather, I prepared them to be out into the world. But then I secreted them away. I hoped his work would continue through his words, which I would memorialize. Yet HaAri understood that his words had the power to destroy if misinterpreted or misused, which was something that I did not want to believe. I could not control what happened upon my death, but my actions had consequences.

PATHS TO UNIFICATION

June 23, 2019

Yes, I have been waiting for you. The pace of these writings will pick up soon, or the work will not get done.

It is with great joy that I can speak and be heard. Yes, others of my era have tried to be heard, but since I am the one who did [most of] the writing and put forth the word to the public to begin with, it is I who must be the one to revise the work and concepts of the time. I will try to speak in the language most relevant to your day and time — in the vernacular, if you will.

You have been researching the significant figures from my time on Earth as Hayyim Vital. It is crucial that you have a context for the people, culture, and history of the time in addition to what I will pass along to you now. The names you discovered are names of those who either shone most brightly or those who most wanted their names to be known. As with all humans, some speak louder than others; some are more brilliant, some are kinder, some are more patient, some more compassionate, and so on.

We were an eclectic group with various experiences, abilities, and points of view, and we came from many places and backgrounds. This may not be so obvious to those who have studied and written about us. Historical accountings mention our religious places of origin [and subsequent places we lived] and our

Torah scholarship. Although our religious roots and scholarship may have brought us together, what held us together was our devotion to connecting with the Divine. We were bound together by our devotion and inspiration to reach out and up to the One and also by our Jewish approach to the quest for ascension and Unification.

Not all streams of Jewish belief were on board with our ways and approaches, not in our day or even in this day. [At times in history, our ways were almost lost.] We operated both within and outside of the normative Judaism of the times. We developed new spiritual technologies born from the depth of Jewish traditions and teachings and also drew from other spiritual paths. Because most of us traveled [between regions and countries] while developing these technologies, we were able to spread our ideas far and wide [at least as far and wide as existed in those times]. Our travels also led us to learn the ways of other religions and cultures.

All technologies must have a core of knowledge upon which they are based. The Essence and Truth of all the teachings we followed are universal, though the specifics are strictly Jewish in tradition and nature. The strong desire that exists within humankind to unite with the Divine is not confined to any one people. Humans have received the wonderful and holy task of finding [and traveling] many roads from many directions and traditions, all to reach the same destination. There are dirt roads, there are paved roads, there are superhighways, and there are many ways between. Some roads are mysterious and less traveled, and some are without signage. Some have many signs along the way, as well as comfort stops and exit signs to facilitate U-turns or to exit the path entirely. In the end, all paths are valid when of pure spirit, heart, and intent.

Not everyone wants to travel these roads, and free will allows us to change our minds [in case we think we want to and then decide against it]. Some are fearless and unrelenting on the journey, and some cannot put even one foot forward without being paralyzed by fear. Such is the journey toward Unification with the Divine.[9]

June 24, 2019

And so, we begin. You have finally noticed the painting of the whirling female Sufi dancer hanging on the wall (above your head) where you have been working almost daily. You see this as both inspired and inspiring, and indeed it is. It is the only art like this here, and it is above your seat. Let us start our own dance and inspiration today.

There are many paths that you will investigate for our work together. The information you glean concerning the different religious pathways to unification with the Divine and religious ecstasy need not be scholarly. **The point of all of this is to espouse simplicity!**

What you have been reading about ecstasy may not always be about Unification with the Divine. Still, it is always about the transcendence of self, for that is true transcendence: expanding outside of one's consciousness. It is not necessarily the Unification of which my colleagues and I spoke. To a degree, it is, but not entirely. There have been many routes to religious ecstasy

---

[9] See "Four Who Entered the Garden" in the Appendix.

throughout the ages, but many have been perverted [corrupted] and glamorized to the point of inauthenticity, even in their intention. The authenticity of a result has everything to do with the [authenticity of the] intent going into an experience. What you put in, you get out.

A more mundane example of intention is the accumulation of wealth. On its face, wealth is neutral, but the intent behind its accumulation determines the spiritual result. Has it been accumulated purely for enjoyment, to present a show to others, or to help those in need and afford a good life for the earner? The one who uses wealth to elevate the lives of others has a more fulfilled soul and greater heartfelt happiness from life in line with love and compassion. If the goal is to become more fulfilled and live a life reflecting divine intention, then the original intent for accumulating wealth does matter. If the motive and intentions are selfish, the person's inner self shall always remain impoverished despite outward appearances.

What of those who pursue religious ecstasy for the sake [the effects] of the experience in and of itself rather than to unify with the Divine for the advancement of the Light and humanity? They will fall short of authentic Unification and mistake their experience for an authentic "merger." Many will be happy with just that since it is enough for them. While their pursuit does not approximate the authentic experience [except on the surface], there is a list of psychological reasons that they find their experience sufficient and seemingly fulfilling. They often teach others in a very loud voice, proclaiming their way as the true and sometimes the only way. You have seen this throughout history and in your present time. There are many purveyors of religious ecstasy and the different roads to it, and they are the ones who are only too eager to share.

Those who genuinely know the road to Unification with the Divine rarely teach it [except by example]. Indeed, they do not widely disseminate the knowledge for fear of it falling into the hands of those who will abuse or misuse it. We never want to think this will happen, but it has, it does, and it will. There is a fair amount written of such occurrences.

It was a great topic of discussion in our group about whether or not to disseminate the information and, if so, in what fashion. A group of us decided together that all of what we had been taught by Isaac Luria would remain with us. In the end, I felt that the world should not forget our work and words, and I chose to commit them to writing. Those who came after me chose to disseminate our work widely, against my and HaAri's wills. I felt that by writing down the brilliance of our master teacher[s], we could preserve the enlightening work to which we had dedicated our lives. Though I was not entirely innocent, I did not believe that our words, thoughts, and practices would or could cause any harm to the world. I was desperate to preserve all our work because I believed in its intellect, power, veracity, and potential. I also believed that it should not die with us.

I must admit that I often could not distinguish my work from that of my esteemed teachers because their words had become so much of a part of me. I may have attributed to them words and thoughts that indeed were my own, and vice versa. The existence and persistence of the Knowledge were all that mattered to me at the time.

June 27, 2019

Well, yes, it is time to work, and today I wish to discuss further the universal basis of truth, which is to say Truth with a capital T. [But I may speak of something appearing to be other than this.] I also want to talk about the universality of the various pathways to the One I mentioned the other day. ["Therefore, my spirit has pressed me to unlock for the *perushim* (seekers), and to support their right hand, to teach them the path to travel." [10]] The more instructions on how to do the dance that leads to the One, the more we know that man is the one who has created the path.

The simpler the path, the more authentic. Authentic connection does not require an elaborate dance or contrived machinations of the mind. Most human beings need instructions on doing things they have never done or directions for going to places they have never been. It is the rare human who at first knows not how and then moves boldly forward, hopefully to the desired result of their efforts. Some enjoy the adventure; they enjoy discovering things for themselves fearlessly. But most humans are fearful, and many are lazy, preferring that others lead the way and create the path. Some need structure and direction and feel comfortable being led, or they will not venture forward on their own. Some will not proceed unless the path is well paved. And some prefer not to dance, not to go forward, but to remain just where they are and learn nothing. All humans have the free [They have chosen the lessons to be learned each lifetime and have the free will to pursue those lessons or not.]

---

[10] Chaim Vital, "Introduction," *Shaarei Kedusha* (*Gates of Holiness*), accessed October 10, 2022, https://www.sefaria.org/Shaarei_Kedusha%2C_Introduction?lang=bi.

But back to the paths to Unification. There are different levels of rising up and a multitude of levels of spiritual ascension. Unification is the highest and most sought-after of these levels, but not entirely accessible or even the most satisfying. This level may be reached for only a fleeting moment before causing damage by having been reached without adequate preparation.[11]

Human beings are called or not called to the task according to the desire and development of their souls. Some desire the extremes of either complete unification or [even] complete rejection of the Divine during their earthly lives. The rest of humanity falls somewhere between the two, as it always has. Please forgive any repetitions of basic knowledge I espouse here, but it is all part of the package I wish to present. Assumptions of the Knowledge often confuse rather than simplify things. So, it is better to say something more than once than have people get lost as they read this.

In my many works, I spoke of those who, in ancient times, were called upon to "touch the Divine" by the Holy Spirit — the breath of God. Then came those who followed in the ways of the prophets. With each descending level, more and more instructions needed to be assembled and put out to those who sought the higher levels. At least, that is how it has been since the days of our fathers and in the ancient times of our primitive history, but not in times before that. [This, too, is a story for another time and not what I want to discuss here.]

The invasion of intellect into matters of spirit complicates things to a great degree. Here, rules and

---

[11] See "Four Who Entered the Garden'" in the Appendix.

regulations arise, and confusion can develop. It is not that the intellect and the spirit are entirely separate but that they each have their purpose, and the blending of the two must be precisely that, a blending. Intellect, ego, and the desire to control — all complicate spiritual matters. While in the world of physical incarnation, it is the intellect that is called upon to obfuscate the spiritual aspect of things. By naming, defining, and verbally regulating the world of spirit, the intellect can keep it under control or even deny it completely. This is not my intended topic here exactly, but perhaps it is in part.

When the path of ascension is populated by words, thoughts, rules, regulations, and signage, it is more effectively blocked than facilitated. This, perhaps, is the gist of my message. In our studies and the development of the spiritual technologies of those times, we attempted to apply the intellectual to the spiritual to a greater degree than was helpful. It is easy to do this for those immersed and well-versed in Torah and Talmudic study. In that mode, it is easy not to even comprehend the lack of others' understanding. Some might feel that those who do not understand should not be told what we know, that they do not know enough, or are not ready. Some of this concern is intellectual snobbery born of ego, and some is genuine concern for the well-being of those who do not understand. But what is it that they do not understand?

MORE ABOUT TRUTH, WISDOM, AND KNOWLEDGE

June 29, 2019

I said I would speak of Truth. I said I would show the way. Historically, it has been difficult to reach people outside their specific tribal cultures unless one uses the language of those [same] cultures. All my work was in the Jewish study tradition: the tradition of learning Torah and Talmud and prayer, the tradition of our sacred language, religion, texts, culture, and history. I learned from great Jewish scholars and holy men. All my life, I lived every moment immersed in Jewish culture, rituals, and customs. At times I had other worldly interests,[12] all seen from the Jewish perspective. So, this is what I knew, and my knowledge and wisdom during my days on Earth came through the lens of all I have mentioned.[13] That lens is still most comfortable to me, even though I now see from a much more universal perspective.

---

[12] I was fascinated by the sciences and especially alchemy. See Eliezer Brodt, "R. Chaim Vital and his Unknown Work Sefer ha-Pe'ulot: A Work on Science, Medicine, Alchemy and Practical Magic," July 8, 2010, accessed October 20, 2022,

I know that Truth belongs to all who desire it. Wisdom can belong to all who seek it. The prerequisites to acquiring Truth, Wisdom, and Knowledge do not and will never belong exclusively to any one tribal domain. One does not need to remove oneself from society to acquire these things. It is of utmost importance that one maintains his standing and place in society to integrate them into human interactions and society in general. And it is also a time in humanity that Truth and Wisdom must be accessible to all [though truthfully, they have always been.]

On another day, I spoke of the potential consequences of coming upon too much knowledge too quickly or prematurely in one's emotional development. Not all humans have reached the stage of development that makes them ready for comprehensive or intensive instruction about the path to the various levels of ascension and unification with the One. But many are ready to hold onto the level they find themselves at and progress according to their desire and abilities. Any flaw in the purity of intent of instruction diminishes the value of such instruction and can harm both student and teacher. Many who know the way lack integrity when they become the purveyor/transmitter of this information. It is only with purity of intent and lack of ego in transmitting the Knowledge that the technology works as intended. You cannot run any technology without the integrity of its most basic elements. Flawed input or equipment will give flawed results. If just one aspect of the machinery is flawed in its manufacture, has

---

https://www.academia.edu/37197602/R_Chaim_Vital_and_his_Unknown_Work_Sefer_ha_Peulot_pdf.

[13] Safed was a major stop on trade routes in the Ottoman Empire, which resulted in its dissemination of other cultures. See "Safed and Rabbinic Biographies" in the Appendix.

MORE ABOUT TRUTH, WISDOM, AND KNOWLEDGE

become worn from mishandling, or is used for other than its intended purpose, then the desired results will not be achieved. Integrity is one of the elements necessary for anything to work [have value] in a lasting and beneficial manner.

Even now, I realize the extent of the limitations of language. Each time I wish to give over an idea, the words do not exactly fit what I want to express to you. Flaws in flow and logic arise. The analogies I am using are modern and not from my previous experience. Again, my goal is to simplify this, so I must step out of my tribal language and references.

To make a point, one must use the language and references of those he addresses. Ah ha! This is also part of what I am passing on to you — it must be made simple and within reach of where each person "stands" and understands! Anyone who attempts the journey without proper intent and preparation will incur damage to himself or others, and anyone who has the desire to ascend must understand not only the way, but the why. Climbing the ladder of ascent to the One requires releasing the ego, letting go of untruths previously accepted as Truth [and beliefs], and balancing one's life in terms of knowledge and emotional maturity.

You will see that not all our topic entries are strictly sequential, and what you think is coming next may not be. What you think may be covered in a transmission may not be. Whatever needs to be said will be said, and whoever needs to know will know. Of this, I am sure. Truth is Truth, but it can be told in many ways, for each mouth speaks according to a person's understanding and ability, and each ear hears and absorbs in its own way and frequency.

Refer later to the work of HaAri and the permutation of the letters, for although the work [to be passed on] was written, its oral transmission was all about vibrational frequency — the sound frequency of the letters. Ah ha! Now you understand the main reason he did not want his work written — sound frequency! The written word cannot convey as accurately as sound. We know words are interpreted and, as such, they can be mistakenly or intentionally misinterpreted. Frequency cannot be misinterpreted. [It can, however, be misused]. Ah ha! We have here another topic, but for another day.

REDEMPTION

June 30, 2019

I spoke of the fact that I did not believe our "technologies" [methods] would be misused, abused, or corrupted in any way. I did not see the dark side. I did not see all the battles that needed to be fought for the victory of good and Light in the world, and I did not see that there would be or had been impediments to gathering the *Klippot*[14] or shards of the broken vessels of which HaAri spoke.

From the Transcriber
There was a sense of urgency amongst the Kabbalists, as well as the general Jewish population, to see the coming of the Messianic age due to a variety of oppressions that had befallen them, most

---

[14] In the traditional sense, *klippot* refers to the broken shards of the vessel in which the Creator sent out the Light. The Light was too great for the vessel and the vessel shattered. It is the work of man to reclaim the vessel's shards, which are interpreted to be the darkness, and free any Light that may be trapped within them. "Literally husk or shell in English the klipah refers to any spiritual blockage preventing us from spiritual growth or transformation." Defined by Rabbi Yosef Karpman, "Klippah," *Atzmut,* accessed January 18, 2023, https://atzmut.net/question/klippah/.

prominently the 1492 Expulsion from Spain. A major objective of the Kabbalists of Safed (and beyond) at that time was to intensify their work to hasten the arrival of the messiah. The Kabbalists of Safed took on the responsibility and moved toward this goal through prayer, practices, and spiritual actions.

They perceived (and rightly so) that there was a great evil in the world and a critical need for something to be done to counteract the dark energies and forces that were so prevalent on Earth. The Lurianic practices that were developed and adopted by many were spiritual technologies to activate the forces of Light (God), which would counteract evil and bring on the messiah. The advent of the messiah would hasten the redemption of the Jewish people and humanity.

July 1, 2019

We shall indeed be discussing some of the exact work to which I would like to put forth revisions and thoughts. [But not today.] There was a tremendous amount of theology, thoughts, practices, and liturgy created in my time, so much so that I cannot use this work alone to focus on it all. Some works will stand as they have for so many centuries without needing revision.

It is common practice for Jewish scholars to comment on the work of others long after the original work has been written or taught [as evidenced in the Talmud and commentaries]. We will focus on the consequences of your present-day world and circumstances, theologies, and technologies [though written long ago]. For today, just as in my time and as you mentioned yesterday, there is a preponderance of dark and prosecutorial energy in your world. Often, the darkness is stirred up and spread maliciously to seem like this is the prevailing condition. But in your world, those who work with the energy of the Light are stronger and more widespread throughout the planet [than at almost any time in history].

There is much more positivity and Light in your world now than you might imagine. It is much more widespread than it was centuries ago. But when this condition prevails, the dark energy seems to grow stronger and louder, even if it is actually diminishing. It is acting up and reacting to the increasingly limited space allotted by the strengthening of the Light. True, it is widespread and virulent, and in significant part amplified due to the modern communication technologies in your world. It is not nearly as strong as it purports itself to be. And so, you see, there must be revisions in techniques to combat this deep infiltration and to see the true size of this rather than the broadcasted version. These same technologies benefit those who work toward redemption as well. That is what we called redemption — deliverance. We are redeemed — or delivered — when we return from darkness to the Light and rescue whatever sparks of Light may be embedded in the darkness [*Klippot*], saving ourselves and others in both body and soul. [We seek redemption from that which has threatened humanity for most of its existence — in one way or another.] We believed, in my day, that each of us, and even more so, all of us collectively, could hasten redemption. We believed our actions would bring the messiah and the Messianic Age to the Earth. Some still believe in the coming of a messiah,[15] and some in the coming of a second messiah.

Our small circle was energetically much larger than just the few humans that inhabited it. We believed we had the power to redeem all humanity, but mostly the Jews because we were the most obviously persecuted [in our eyes and to our knowledge]. We believed our words and our actions could and would bring about great things. Through meditation [extremely specific types of meditation, some possibly to be discussed], prayer, and action [also to be discussed], we believed we could affect a "shift," as you call it.

Although we were a small circle, we were, as I said, diverse, as diverse as any group of people who work together for a common cause. We were drawn together by the holy nature of the work, and even though we may have followed one teacher or another, many of us also had our own ideas. With all the learning in my life and the Knowledge I possessed, I was a devotee of the masters, not believing myself to be on their level. I felt this way despite being a leader in the community, defined by my role as the one who served to [legitimately] chronicle the teachings of the masters, along with my other roles. I do admit that I was initially partly drawn in by the charismatic nature of those I considered to be masters. How could one help but be swept up in the holy swirl of energy that surrounded them? I also believed in their ideas and admired their mastery of our traditions. I did have ideas of my own, and after the passing of HaAri, I included them in my writings and teachings. Oh, I suffered great loss upon his passing,

---

[15] The promised deliverer of the Jewish nation prophesized in the Hebrew Bible.

as did we all, and so soon after the loss of our previous master teacher, the RaMaK. It was often difficult to go on without them. Their teachings and Light stayed with us and kept them with us in a fashion.

It was my role to make sure the teachings were recorded with accuracy and integrity. In this way, they remained with us and gained a reputation and influence by virtue of this association. Personal memories and public legends also kept them present in our lives and culture. What a turning point it was in our history and beliefs.

The RaMaK had redacted the first accepted systemization of Kabbalah based on its rational categorization and study. This was an innovation, a brilliant and well-accepted first, which had been achieved in learning and disseminating Kabbalah using what was known on the topic up until that point in time. Isaac Luria had a different approach with completely new doctrines and some reinterpretations of what had been previously revealed. Cordovero did not innovate as much as he systematized and documented. In time, the Lurianic school of Kabbalah emerged as the dominant system; however, the works of the RaMaK are still highly esteemed and widely studied.

There was not merely a transition in leadership but in theology, practices, and how we worked toward our goal. Both Cordovero and Luria were taken from us too soon. Their lights had shone so brightly yet for so short a time. Perhaps that is why they could stay with us no longer than they did. The changes and shifts that came upon the RaMaK's passing allowed for a necessary forward movement, though we were not necessarily aware of this immediately. It was like advancements you experience today, which occur very quickly in the scheme of things. With such seamlessness, you do not always realize what is happening until you look back upon it from a historical perspective. The last device or innovation seems fine and adequate until the next one comes along, the one you did not know you needed, and you slide into the use of the new thing as though it had always been there. There are many stories about this succession, and it seemed a natural progression for us.

During the time of the RaMaK, I followed his presence, his scholarship, and his confident leadership. His position as our circle's leader was not left open for more than the blink of an eye before being assumed by HaAri, whose arrival in Safed was perfectly timed so that there was no break in the community between the ways of the RaMaK and HaAri. Such was the gift and the charisma of our new leader. Really, at the time and upon reflection from a higher perspective, it was all perfect. He had come to Safed at the behest of his guide, the Prophet Elijah, and at Elijah's behest, he sought me out.

July 2, 2019

From the Transcriber

R. Hayyim assured me of his presence while I read from Gershom Sholem's book tracing Luria's authentic writings. He laughed at his occasional uncertainty about information that belonged to him and what he learned from his teachers. On a more serious note, he asserted, "Energy was created in that time and location beyond the members of the community and its luminaries."

You are making interesting discoveries outside the information you are receiving from me, which is good; it will widen the scope of this work. There is much that is tangential to the information I will give you, and it will be helpful for you to have a more comprehensive understanding of what we are doing and the context and depth of the material. More than just my remembrances and revisions of my work, you will be given further insights and valuable tools to pass on.

July 3, 2019

And we begin. I will first discuss more of the setting, the times, and my perspective on them.

When I was a student of the RaMaK, we learned together as I sat at his feet. There was so much to learn from him. I also was given Wisdom and Knowledge from other sources that contributed to our learning together. The others who were involved in our learning (those of my time and circle who, incidentally, would also like to speak with you) felt they had something to say, but this is my work with you, so I will prevail for now. [I already had guides that gave me the information I needed, but I did not speak with them because I was unsure about the origins of what I was hearing. It was not a dialogue with my guides at that point. I listened but did not speak directly to them.]

Although the RaMaK was a master of the sacred Knowledge and given the greatest share of it, he was always open to listening to his students, some more than others. Despite his masterful teachings and writings, he was a man of great humility. I knew him to be kind and compassionate and open to listening to points of view that were not his own, but he did not take well to those who sought to usurp his knowledge publicly or acted with *hubris*. In the pursuit of high levels of knowledge and the lofty nature of our work, *hubris* comes quickly and easily to those who are out of balance in their minds and emotions. I feel that his steady and loving hand with me prevented me from this, though there are others who no doubt would take issue with that statement.

In the company of HaAri [I have to say], we walked more as partners [as much as anyone could be with him]. We shared more "experientially," as is the current term. The practices and the way in which we observed the world were the core of how we related to one another. It was as if I was so completely drawn in by the magical nature of all that existed in his world that my feet often did not touch the ground. In my eyes, and in the eyes of so many others, his feet did not walk on the same ground as the rest of us. It seemed he was not of this world. He seemed to live in a vastly different spiritual world than the rest of us. The experiences we shared lasted throughout my lifetime, though sadly in diminishing degrees. As you know, I had a long life.

The effects of our experiences endured in our world and with me, and that is what carried me through many difficult times that followed. Remembering flashes and moments of ascension and transcendence kept me strong inside and gave me sustenance in my weaker moments. His words and experiences drew my attention to those I otherwise would have missed. His friendship bolstered me in difficult times. Keeping up his legacy was a challenge I took very seriously. No two people remember things in the same way, but there should not be animosity about what we recall. And yet there was. Even in the glow of Love, Light, and enlightenment, my human ego, immaturity, and personal shortcomings sometimes interfered, as there were arguments as to many aspects of his legacy of teachings and practices. As I mention elsewhere in these pages, the teachings were such that each of us understood at his capacity, and that varied. Since he did not write down his teachings, differences of interpretation were rampant. But we all saw the miracle of his life in much the same way.

We were to bring on the advent of the messiah and the Messianic Age, where all would be well. But it was not well. All I can say is that I did my best, but as I look back, it was not always seen as such by others. I had the learning and the Knowledge and hopefully some Wisdom. Still, I did not have the charismatic nature of the masters whose paths I followed. No matter how closely I may have followed their words and put forth the lessons of my teachers, it was never the same. [HaAri himself came to me after his death to remind me of his exact words and intentions and show me where I may have erred.]

Some of the disciples remained, some became traveling teachers and spread the word, and some fell off the path, losing the glue that came from the master's charisma. Teachings were passed on but only with the understanding [and limitations] of the one who had learned. What I mean is that students were only capable of understanding given each one's bestowed and allowed abilities. I will say the result was not always the teaching as it was intended or how even I understood it.

Looking back, I saw myself as the ruthless guardian of the precious Knowledge of the RaMaK and HaAri, and I was convinced that only my understanding of their teachings was correct. Although, in essence, I still believe this, I can see a need for different interpretations and points of view so that people at varying levels of comprehension all have an opportunity to relate to the essence on some level. I regret this was not something I had come to then. [I am, from my current perspective, displeased with my lack of compassion at that time in this regard, which reflects the presence of ego.] Not everyone is on the same level. The truth is that no one is ever on the same level as anyone else. That is something we must always keep in mind. It is sometimes a hard-learned lesson that led me to some bitterness in my lifetime, and in truth and retrospect, it diminished the holiness of my work in my eyes.

If we do not live as we teach, then we are lost to the heights we wish to attain. We cannot simultaneously aspire to lofty levels and be in the ego of rightness. Well, we can aspire to, but we cannot achieve what we seek. This is one of the dangers of knowing too much before one is ready. The complex intellectual concepts and ideas can be put forth but cannot be genuinely understood without letting go of rightness and egotistical possession of the Knowledge. Compassion and generosity of spirit are essential parts of the package.

Many times, I forgot that these are essential parts of the teachings. Most of us did, for we did not have the qualities of our teachers that allowed them to operate on such a level.

July 4, 2019

We continue today where we left off yesterday.

I was not always sure of why I held tightly to my understanding of what was taught to me, which I taught to a select few others and included in my transcriptions. Writing the words down as quickly and accurately as possible would give me the freedom to decide later. I did not want the teachings to be lost, yet I did not know if I was wise to pass them along to a larger audience. The misfortune [in my eyes] was that others took it upon themselves to make my decision for me. They stole my property [the manuscripts] and disseminated my work without my permission. The lack of integrity in their actions led to a lack of integrity and accuracy in copying my work. Had it been done with my consent, I would have seen to the integrity of the copies made and maintained control over the distribution of the work.

I could be fooling myself. It is well recorded that I was in a state of severe illness when the documents were removed from my home to be copied for a fee. When greed is the operating impetus, things rarely go well. And they did not. I do not want to dwell on interpretations of my original teachings, but what I wrote was either deliberately or carelessly or ineptly corrupted. The end result was the end result, no matter what the intent.

Corrupted copies of my writings made it out into the world, and I was not happy when I regained my health and learned of this. I thought if I could lock up my writings, I would one day find the right person or persons to whom I could entrust them. But I had my work stolen from me more than once. I did not learn. I would not let go. I tried to control everything, from the way the teachings were interpreted to who should receive them. **When one cannot give up control, it is usually wrested from them.**

I now know that sometimes control must be taken away from a person or stolen by the universal forces that know better than man. Maybe by exerting extreme focus on or control over a topic, we bring on the very event we fear. Now I will tell you, reveal to you that part of the control I exerted was due to insecurity, not bravado. [The insecurity was due to my fear of misusing words, of not getting it all just right, and of what might arise if the materials got out and into the hands of the wrong person. Disaster might ensue whether I got it all right or not.]

As for the work of others, mostly HaAri, I feared I may have gotten something slightly wrong, and that is something for which I never forgave myself. As for my work, I feared I might not have been perfectly correct in my postulations. I am sure that no one knew this at the time. The work we did was precise and unbelievably powerful. One whisper in the wrong direction or a misplaced word or letter could influence things with an unintended trajectory, resulting in who knows what end. That is what I thought. That is what I was sure I understood. I am not sure how much superstition, yes superstition, was involved. Or was it fear of getting something wrong? I did not fear others so much. But I was unsure how to proceed.

July 5, 2019

Now, it may seem that from time to time, I mention something and then appear to forget about that subject. But I do not. To whoever reads my words, I tell you that I will return at some point to each of the topics I mentioned, whether in this volume or another. Please do not be sidetracked by what you may think is absentmindedness or a lack of memory or logic flow on my part. I am aware that even though I mention something in a particular context, it may not necessarily be the best moment to expound upon it. Perhaps I am more occupied with the flow of events, having the reader experience me, and getting out the story rather than inserting commentaries. The commentary on rituals, practices, and theories will be in separate chapters or perhaps in another book.

July 7, 2019 (Take 2)

From the Transcriber
The original transmission for this day was lost due to a technical issue. I have attempted to recover as much as possible in this "Take 2."

For now, let us recall the essence of the message. Humans have infinite resources within them to live their missions in this world and to fulfill their roles, attaining the ultimate goal of their lifetimes. This goal is to restore the Light and the Love necessary to raise the [spiritual] level of all life on the planet. It sounds like a daunting task if each human tries to do this by taking on the role of another. Yet this comes with ease when we are in harmony with the Source within us instead of "wrestling" what we experience when we endeavor to take on the role designated to another. [Be yourself, and, in doing that, your role is much easier to fulfill. If you find life difficult, it is most likely you are not being true to yourself (your essence).]

When we do not sit comfortably within the seat of our souls, we begin to struggle and live in discord. We cannot comprehend what comes from higher sources or realms when we attempt to hear with the ears of another. We will never comprehend efficiently if we pursue that road. We can only hear the song we are meant to hear in this life through our own ears, at our own level, and with our own soul. Otherwise, the sound and the message will be corrupted. The beauty and authenticity of the message, song, or learning will neither benefit the listener nor those to whom it is passed. This was the cause of the conflict and strife in my day but is not confined to that time [of course]. However, it must also be said that the corruption of the learnings, the message, the ensuing, and the end results of that behavior are also part of the learning.

So, you see, the trajectory one takes will go in a specific direction that leads to the subsequent trajectory, which is not necessarily where one would have landed if a different course had been taken. No step one takes is independent of the last or the next. There is an ideal that each person lives within their perfect self, according to the vibration of their soul, accessing their highest potential of inner resources. An infinite variety of paths can occur depending upon what level is actualized by an individual. The major factors in reaching one's maximum potential of inner power are intention and the degree of ego that enters a person's thoughts and actions. Both can easily be influenced by the environment [of people and places]. The intention and the integrity of one's desire determine the degree of access to the Divine self.

JOY

July 9, 2019

I would like to speak to you today about Joy. It is incumbent upon each person to know how to create and enjoy an easier, more joyful, and fulfilling life that feels natural and flowing without fighting and tension. To achieve this state, one needs to be in the company of other humans and [re]sources that support the desire to live a "good" and happy life. More likely, throughout most of our lives, we find ourselves in the company of humans who do not support this desire and are not on the quest to be who they are meant to be [their authentic, essential self].

The greatest joy I felt in my lifetime was in the company of HaAri and from memories of our experiences and the moments we spent together learning, talking, praying, and exploring new theories and levels of consciousness. And then there were the moments we spent laughing. Laughing did not come easily to me, but his spirit was Light and so aligned with his Creator that laughter sprung from him most naturally, sometimes like a bubbling brook and sometimes like a glorious fountain that spread its joy to everyone in its vicinity. I did not achieve that lightness of spirit in my lifetime, but I often recalled his laughter, which lifted me up. I wish that I had been able to engage in more laughter in my lifetime, but that was not to be. That was not who I was meant to be, but I did so enjoy laughter for a short time.

Those were the moments I lived with complete integration of the essence I learned in his presence. He introduced me to things, even the simplest sights of the everyday world, through the perspective and lens he looked through. His magic [his nature] was contagious, and, by example, he led those near his being to lift themselves into the [elevated] world that surrounded him. That world was one of intense connection with the One. It was so intense that the air around him often seemed to shimmer and vibrate — somewhat like the air of a scorching day but without the heat and with more sparkle. This was Joy, and these moments existed out of time or space as we know it to be [and usually experience it]. There were moments similar to some I experienced in prayer or meditation from time to time, but the truth is that neither prayer nor meditation was needed to achieve them. When I was with him, I lost sight of what I had considered my role in life, a role assigned and imposed by all those around me and which I took on dutifully all my life. My happiest times were when I lived in those moments of having released my assigned role. I was simply experiencing the wonders of life according to what was shown me by HaAri when I was my essential self. These were not necessarily new experiences but rather [as I mentioned] experiences seen through a new lens.

I assumed, at the time, that his learning, theories, and practices created his magic. That was my main reason for taking on the task of recording them for the future. I took on the act of recording these things for myself as much as for others. I took it very seriously since I thought that following the teachings and the practices was the way to the joy and the glorious state I had experienced with HaAri. But I will tell you now that I know this to be a different story. He carried his magic inside of him — not just in his mind or his words, but within all the levels of his soul and every cell of his human self.

I regret to say that the initial level of joy I experienced with him never returned to me for the rest of my days. I occupied myself with the profoundly serious business of getting it "all right," of recording accurately and recreating the rituals and practices precisely. I did this to the degree that obliterated the space the joy had occupied. I suffered physically for many years, and I suffered in my spirit. I had ceased to live what we had experienced together, what I knew to be the true path in life. I left the real work for what *I thought* was the real work. You see, the old paradigm of an intellectual approach to spirituality still reigned in the culture, and without my lifeline to the true way, I fell into the consciousness of the world and the culture around me.

There were moments of enlightenment, but they were difficult to sustain on my own. I made progress, but nothing compared to before. It was as though a pendulum had swung far in one direction, and the swing to the other extreme was in progress but happening slowly. Only when I did the work and the practices *with the imprint of joy I had experienced in his presence years before* did I feel full connection and happiness once again. Of course, from my current perspective, I now see the experience of my lifetime differently than when I was in it; now, it is from a perspective of seeing it in its entirety. I do have the ability to visit specific experiences, but now I see the big picture. And I regret the moments my sorrow rejected the potential for experiencing joy when it presented itself.

Even with our devotion to learning and our commitment to our work, it was a constant test of the human self to battle with the ego. When in battle, one cannot be in joy [for one must surrender to be in joy]. Some of this was due to being left in a bit of a void after the last two giants we had learned with, Moses Cordovero and Isaac Luria, passed on. For those of us whose feet still touched the ground, it was easier to trip and fall, often over our own feet. Commitment can sometimes be misassigned or delegated [by the self], or misaligned. We sometimes commit to the work but not the true goal of the work, which is connection and the joy in that connection. [This is what I meant when I said I left the True path for what I thought was true.] If we find ourselves without the humor, lightness, and experience that connects us to the world above and the world below, then we are lost to the Truth and the accompanying Joy (which is another of the intended goals of life in physical form).

Most of our practices were designed to elevate a person by means of enacting those practices. But we did not foresee the limitations of those who were not us, though perhaps we should have [even if some of them were among our numbers]. We could not see the potential that our practices held for the future. Rather than as aids in the ascension of human consciousness and spirit, they were too often seen merely as obligations and traditions that would be-recited by rote and which would restrict what one *must say and do*. And so, they lost their intrinsic meaning and purpose [and joy]. When our work was performed with the abandonment of worldly thoughts, and we had no other focus than joy and service to the One [Source] who directed everything, then the Light and Love created by our actions illuminated the world and us as well.

Without the charisma, leadership, and loving attention of our compelling earthly guides, we often lost our way. In our fervor to pass on what we had learned [or what we perceived we had learned], we sometimes elevated our egos to a level where the point [joy] was lost. Each was convinced that his perceptions of the teaching were correct. I have to say, each had an earthly desire to follow the path and role of HaAri as closely as possible, yet that is when the ego took over. Each of us was also convinced of our power and rightness of action as the result of our zeal to continue what our teachers had established. There was no joy in any of that. We did not even see what we had lost through the intensity of our quest to hold on to it. Such intense desire emanating from the ego can aid the elusive nature of the object of desire.

We did not focus enough on the joy itself but on its creation rather than just feeling and experiencing joy from the inside. As we found ourselves individually in such states, we discovered [though not always consciously] that we were no longer the supportive communities I mentioned earlier in this transmission. The community's fractures were antithetical to our work and took a toll on the levels of work and spirituality [Light] we were able to produce. Yes, we each had support, but the initial group had fractured, wreaking havoc with our desired results.

Joy can certainly be experienced alone. However, our individual spirit can be enhanced by a like-minded group or depleted when a formerly supportive group is no more. Not that all went to seed, but we could have done better. We could have done more, especially since one of our main goals was to bring on the messiah's arrival. [I ask you, was that a time for the intrusion of ego? It was, it seems, a time for the lesson of allowing ego to interfere with a greater mission.]

It was a glorious time, yet there was the potential for it to have shone more brightly had we continued as we were. But that was not to be, although that is the test after all, isn't it — to continue to be the Light, the Joy, the Love, even when [and perhaps, especially when] conditions are not *ideal*? Allow the Light within you to lead rather than assign that role to another human. *When the leader is no longer in place and conditions are no longer ideal, what do you do? That is real proof of learning!*

It seems now that humanity resists [and sometimes even retreats] once a certain level of Light is created amongst it. That is to say, a fear of sorts is created and spreads in nefarious ways until it affects even the most ardent proponents of spreading the Light, or, perhaps, especially them. Look at your world now. There are fractures even in the communities that shine most brightly. Leaders and incentivized group efforts are discredited and reputations irreparably damaged so that positively motivated efforts may fail. The fight against the Light has been perpetuated in this way throughout history. When the Light shines too brightly, forces emerge to distract, pervert, and sometimes even destroy it. In your time, this happens, but there are now methods that perpetuate individuals' efforts to change the world — to change the world in the direction of their choice. There are electronic technologies as well as spiritual technologies that aid in these efforts. I have strayed from my topic of Joy, but we will continue in the pursuit of recapturing it.

July 10, 2019

We will continue today with Joy. Yes, that is amusing. We will discuss Joy, and we will do it from a place of Joy. *Avodah Simcha* (Joyful Service) is what we will do. One of the secrets to a happy life is doing service in Love and Joy.

You are correct. You hear my thoughts when you read background material, and I let you know what merits commentary. You read now about the methods and practice of *Yichudim* [Unifications] created by the Arizal [HaAri], and you hear me almost laugh and tell you he needed none of these things to achieve a state of *Yichud* [Unification]. He created all of it because it was a beautifully constructed pathway for those who needed a paved road to reach this state. To repeat a favored analogy: some will reach their destination through a path in the woods or create their own path, some will need at least a well-worn dirt road, and some will require a paved road on which others will only travel if they see others on the road and the signposts clearly marked.

My master needed neither road nor path for him to reach his destination. He had to do no more than have the desire to be there, and he arrived. Such was his state of elevated consciousness. [He was a disciple of Elijah, who often came to him to guide him through his life. Perhaps he traveled to the high places in the chariot of Elijah. This is a fanciful thought on my part but may ring true to some degree.] I did not need a preprinted map either. I did not know that in the early stages.

Other members of our circle were gifted in different ways and to varying degrees. Some had only the gifts of desire and love in their hearts. [Love surpasses all other gifts for the abilities and gifts are activated to their highest levels by the element of Love.] All were welcome to travel to achieve *Yichud* or any level on the way to it. The paths HaAri created for all were placed before them so that they would have clear signs and guideposts on the way.

July 12, 2019

From the Transcriber
R. Hayyim recalled what he knew of the HaAri's birth in great detail. I've included a synopsis of what he shared below from a printed version he led me to.

━━━━━◆━━━━━

A Special Sandek (Godfather)

There was once a very pious scholar living in Israel, named Rabbi Shlomo Luria. One day he remained in the study hall alone, learning, when Elijah the Prophet appeared to him and said, 'I have been sent to you by the Almighty to bring you tidings that your wife shall conceive and bear a child, and that you must call him Yitzchak [Isaac]. He shall begin to deliver Israel from the *kelipot* ['husks,' forces of evil]. Through him, numerous souls will receive their Tikkun [rectification]. He is also destined to reveal many hidden mysteries in the Torah and to expound on the Zohar. His fame will spread throughout the world. Take care, therefore, that you do not circumcise him before I come to be the sandek [the one who holds the child during the circumcision ceremony].'

He finished speaking and disappeared. Rabbi Shlomo Luria went home but did not reveal this secret to anyone, not even to his wife. When Shlomo's son was born, the house was filled with light, and on the eighth day, the child was brought to the synagogue to be circumcised. Shlomo searched everywhere to see if Elijah had come as promised, but he did not see him. Everyone was urging the father to proceed, but he replied that not all the guests had yet arrived.

An hour went by, but Elijah still did not come. Another hour went by, but Elijah still did not come. Then he thought bitterly to himself: My sins must have prevented him from fulfilling his promise. But as he was crying, Elijah appeared and said, 'Do not cry, servant of God. Draw near unto the altar and offer your son as a pure sacrifice dedicated entirely to Heaven. Sit on my chair, and I shall sit upon you.' Whereupon, invisible to everyone present except Rabbi Shlomo, Elijah sat on his lap, received the child with both hands, and held him during the entire circumcision. Neither the mohel [the one who performs the circumcision] nor those assembled saw anything but the father holding his baby. After the circumcision, the Prophet Elijah again promised Rabbi Shlomo that the child would bring great light to the entire world, and then he disappeared.[16]

---

[16] Moshe Miller, "The Holy Ari," *Chabad.org: Kabbalah Online*, accessed August 30, 2022, https://www.chabad.org/kabbalah/article_cdo/aid/380758/jewish/The-Holy-Ari.htm.

And so goes this story of foretelling and the birth and the naming of Yitzchak Luria ben Shlomo Ashkenazi. The Prophet Elijah followed him all the days of his life and lived with him in every breath he took, so much so that it was evident to those around him that his being was bejeweled in some way. The glow of Light in which he walked and spoke and accompanied his thoughts was something that could not be missed, even by those who did not know him. His soul shone quite enough on its own, but with the additional guidance and presence of our prophet Elijah, even more so. It did not just radiate to those in his circle but to anyone who encountered him or who was within the large radiance of his presence and field of energy.

I know that I was one of the most affected by his Light, but that did not blind me to the effect it had on others. It was exceptional and like nothing that any of us had ever previously [or since] witnessed in this world. It sounds like something that is the stuff of legends and created "truths" that only slightly resemble the facts — but I swear to you that this is true to the maximum degree. Could it be just my earthly memory that helped to create the radiance of which I speak? Perhaps a bit, but my memory was corroborated by others who witnessed it as well. Was this radiance within him from the time of his birth? Did it grow through his studies? Did the radiance increase when he joined us in the holy space of Safed, where it could be recognized and honored? I think that all of these statements are true.

I believe the tale I just put forth demonstrates a pattern with humans of great luminescence throughout history. For if a great Light shines too soon or in less-than-optimal surroundings [and by this, I mean any place that is less receptive to the Light — not a place that is elevated to a higher vibration], the human will not be allowed to continue the journey [and will be destroyed by any one of several methods]. At birth, they must have enough Light to be recognized by those who need to do so. The same is true as they mature. Those who can assist in the journey will see as they need to and will assist in the development of this vessel of Light. It is not until a person arrives in the right place, time, and company of receptive people that he will be appropriately received and the full-on radiance of the human allowed to be witnessed or perceived. With some, the nascent, original Light is not nourished or allowed to develop, and so it never develops as it might have. Also, a Light that shines too brightly too soon will be summarily dismissed by the world or even extinguished because it is more than most people can bear.

My Light [for example] was recognized enough to draw the attention of my parents and teachers, who nurtured it. I was allowed to grow and develop and come to live the life that I was directed and privileged to live and to carry forth not only my own Light and Truth but also that of others. [Yes, I was, as you would say, a good guy, but my life with all this responsibility was not an easy one. No doubt my life looks better as one sees it from a distance. True, I was a bit difficult to deal with, but still a good person. What some judged in my behavior to be born of ego was quite the opposite, as it was based on my unsureness that I would not live up to what had been forecasted for me.] None of it was easy, save for a few blinks of an eye during my time spent with HaAri. There was some joy at other times as well during my days on Earth, but after his passing, I spent too much time feeling as though I had been dropped from a great height, and only his teachings and my writings brought back the soaring moments and held me in the space of greater peace and comfort than in any other part of my life. Sadly, the heights I achieved sometimes left in their wake deep depression and sadness that lasted for longer periods than the joy.

I will continue this line of thought, which strays from the topic with which we started today. Conflict can arise when — well, conflict is always [almost always] the result of ego. When a brilliant Light comes into the world of those who had thought of themselves as a brilliant Light, they recognize that they do not shine as brightly as they [or most of them] had believed. Of course, they had never shone as brightly as they believed because their egos were more in the forefront than their Light. What they projected as a great magnitude of brilliance was false. [The one who shines the brightest knows it quietly (if he knows it) and does not speak of it.] These people do not take kindly to the diminishment of what they had thought to be the Truth [especially their personal truth], and they can react in a manner that can be quite disruptive. I am not saying any specific names, but when the history is read and the story told, the Truth will be known.

Truth is what is important, not names. Although the names will change throughout history, the patterns will remain. It is about this I wish to speak now. The true bearer of the greatest Light does not see himself as such. It is possible that the bearer may recognize his true nature, but with humility. And no other being is diminished or less than, in their sight. The true bearer of the great Light wears the mantle [both inner and outer] gently and in peace, distributing the benefits and gifts from the Light easily, with compassion and joy.

Jewish tradition says that Elijah comes to each child when brought into the covenant as it is written,[17] but he resides to a greater degree with some than with others as their lives progress. With whom he continues to live may be by providence or merit. Some humans remember and long for the Light that once burned more brightly within them. They do not recognize, understand, or accept the role of merit [or providence] in determining the chosen. Those who wish for their Light to burn brighter can achieve this. Still, as I have stated and will state again: the intention and integrity of their desire are the most significant determining factors in selecting the chosen.

———◆———

You notice once again that the various things to which your attention is drawn in the world these days are connected to this work we are doing together. You wonder about the influences that you see and read about my work, but you must also realize that you are directed to these seeming distractions for exposure to topics and ideas that I may discuss. They help you understand and give you new perspectives. You may be assured that you are not

---

[17] "The tradition is to designate a chair for Elijah the Prophet, the 'Angel of the Covenant,' at every circumcision. Many synagogues have an ornamental chair for this purpose. Some have the custom that the sandek, the one holding the child on his lap during the circumcision, sits on this chair. Others use a chair that is wide enough for both the sandek and Elijah."
See Dovid Zaklikowski, "The Chair of Elijah and Welcoming the Baby," *Chabad.org*, accessed 8/27/2020,
https://www.chabad.org/library/article_cdo/aid/144123/jewish/The-Chair-of-Elijah-and-Welcoming-the-Baby.htm.

infusing your own opinions or information into this transmission. Ideas have been introduced to you so that you will be familiar with the subject when it comes up. Please pay attention to how this happens in life. When many things of the same ilk come to you, pay attention, for there is a message to be derived from these occurrences. They are not random.

SPIRITUAL TECHNOLOGIES

July 15, 2019

In your research, you are on the trail of one who has written from a consciously academic viewpoint. This individual is unaware of how he has been guided to do all he discovers. It is "in his blood," he will say. He, too, has come to clarify many of our ideas and concepts and give them form, which is only possible by intellectually and academically recalling and recovering the informational materials. For most, communication cannot be direct and conscious [as in the case of these transmissions]. There are misrepresentations and inaccuracies due to the interference of the ego, as there were in our time and as there have always been.

    I speak to you at times as myself alone [if that is indeed possible], but you noticed that I just said "we," and you wonder when I refer to "we" and "us." You previously mentioned the Oversoul. Remember? To explain initially and simply (an in-depth explanation will come later), each individual belongs to a larger group of souls who, in turn, are a part of the Oversoul. When you are overloaded with frequency and information in such a way (due to the intensity of the Oversoul), it is helpful to no one, and we wish you to recognize this state and learn to ask to turn down the frequency. Your mind can manage it, but your body cannot.

From the Transcriber
I have questions based on some of what I have been reading. Why would God deny the Light to any given space or person? Is that the meaning of the absence of Kedusha (holiness)? Or is it that a person who shuts out the Light through his own will or actions? And then why would a place be without Light? Is it possible for anything to even exist without the Light?

All creation has Light upon its inception, as its very source is Light. All creations also include a tiny space without measurable Light. Depending upon the person's will or environment, and on their will and actions — yes, upon their will and actions — the measures of Light and darkness vary. The Force, The Creator, The Source, The One — denies nothing to his creations. It is in the realm of free will that the negative, the darkness, enters. The further from its connection with the glory of creation, the more the darkness seeps into the space where the Light is denied. This feeds upon itself, and so the negative and darkened space grows. We repeat that no place or being is without any *Light,* or it would cease to be.

This, as you see, is quite a simple answer rather than the volumes of answers provided in today's world and throughout history. In the same way, the mysteries, or so-called mysteries that reveal themselves to those who desire Knowledge, contain all manner of explanations. These explanations may be tedious and may or may not make sense to some, depending upon their level of understanding and acceptance. The revelation of these mysteries is best achieved without words, but that is not what those who inquire request. They would prefer words that they cannot truly comprehend rather than consult [acquaint themselves with] the energies that might relate the mysteries in more efficient ways.

Curiosity exists, but the one who consults and inquires without fear is taken to the place of true Understanding, a place without the construct of words. And so, the volumes written cannot serve as viable and understandable explanations of the mysteries themselves but only as a vehicle for those willing to go beyond the words and the concrete concepts "of the mind." The words (as well as sounds and vibrations) are a key, a trigger, which releases the lock on the limited mindset and allows for what is beyond human explanation. Even those who have learned the mysteries and understand them [within human capacities] cannot give a complete or accurate intellectual explanation of what they know. They do not have the words to explain, so many treatises on the mysteries are incomprehensible to most. These writings, however, if genuine, contain keywords that trigger the release of the logical mind so that it may open enough to allow in as much as the human mind can integrate.

I now know that all Knowledge is a gift to the receivers of it. It is gifted according to the level that they are capable of understanding. Not all selected recipients choose to respond to the call. This is not an issue; it is what you sometimes call a gamble, and we are ready to allow acceptance or rejection [whether conscious or unconscious]. I will tell you that a human mind is receptive to the knowledge that comes to it at a specific time in life when an individual is ready and most open to it. If the mind is unprepared, the intended recipient will either be closed off from or so open to the Knowledge that either condition can destroy the individual's ability to survive in the world.

Some have a proclivity for certain understandings over others and will be more predisposed to picking up on the practical nature of what is passed on to them. It is natural and intuitive, and they do not need instruction in this world. If others also understand and have experience, they may assist one who wishes to but does not yet understand. If one who "knows" can pass on the smallest information of this gift, it may remind others to seek out what they are destined to know; this also is permissible — or, let us say, likely to occur. It is potentially dangerous to thrust knowledge upon one not naturally predisposed to that knowledge.

I can see that explaining the simplicity of all this may seem confusing. That is somewhat laughable to both of us. Why would I want to explain things to you if they are so simple? But really, why would I want to give simplified answers to you if they would, in the end, cause even more confusion? Ah, this is the question. And this is also a difficulty throughout history.

It is time for me and some others to come forth and explain a few things so that the formulaic teachings of the past can be released into the ether. It is not that they have no relevance whatsoever, for historically, they do. Your age has so many technologies. Most use some form of artificial intelligence, and the technologies depend on the technical skills and physical elements needed to build them. I have spoken of technologies of the past — the ways of accessing the mysteries of life and the universe. These also rely on what some may consider artificial bits of intelligence [in a way] and are difficult to access. [Why would you choose to use a supercomputer when now your phone could do the job for you? Times change; technology changes. Technologies change and simplify life for the user. The destination does not change, just the method of transportation.]

Your world has reached a point when humanity must quickly come to a new understanding in much the same way that my world needed to create new inroads to access the messiah and the Messianic Age. We were not successful in bringing that about, as we were under the false impression that the actualization of the messiah could be achieved by just a few humans harnessing cosmic powers. For all the power we could access and all the techniques we developed and perfected, it was beyond what a few accomplish.

We were wrong in our assumptions and beliefs that such powers were limited to those who might have access to such a small group. We needed the abilities of an exceptionally large number of humans working to harness the powers and the Light necessary to bring about what we called redemption.

For the Messianic Age to materialize, most of humanity must choose to participate in the behaviors that would bring about the level of Light and Love in the world to make this happen. Only a few may initiate the process, but nearly all must participate.

The call is out on many fronts, in many languages and formats, and by many teachers in recent years. I am here with you to broaden and embolden the call. It must be put out in many spheres of society and in many ways. Those who are ready will access what they need to know. We are all here, ready to broadcast to those who will respond to the call *in language they will understand*.

SHIFTING PERSPECTIVES AND PERCEPTIONS

July 16, 2019

At the beginning of this project, I proposed that this was to be a revision of some of my works and ideas, and so it shall be in part. All thoughts develop, change, and shift into what they must be in the end rather than as conceptualized in their beginning. If we stay with the original concept, the material might seem a bit dry and forced. I, indeed, might wander back into my overly academic, detailed, and restrictive pathway since it is easy to fall into old patterns — even with this new and "celestial" perspective [for one's character is one's character]. Other things are more important than merely the revision of my work as it stands, and we shall discuss these things in addition to what I originally intended.

Since I first called upon you, things have changed in your world enough so that our work, too, must change. When I first spoke to you, or rather when I first got your attention, the world situation had not yet bubbled up to the surface as it has now. There was not yet the level of constant and incessant global communication. This is a major contributing factor to the urgency of remediation of the troublesome issues. It works toward the spread of darkness, but also toward the spread of Light. Throughout time, there has been evil [the absence of Light], oppression, torture, murder, unkindness, and all manner of human energy and actions run amuck. There have also been compassion, kindness, and selfless Light-filled acts alive and functioning among the planet's inhabitants. The balance has shifted back and forth, both in actuality and in the minds of humans. Why is this? Free will is the cause of all darkness, as is the lack of conscious choice to be in the Light.

When humans cast their darkness out into the world,[18] the darkness can take the form of sadness, or pain, or cruelty [physical or mental], and, in abundance, it can begin to tip the balance when the free will of the masses has chosen to remain without consciousness about what is befalling them. To put it more simply, one who does not take charge and make conscious choices can be easily swayed and brought into a flow that is not their own — even without their conscious awareness. Few humans know that they are using their free will when they choose to live in darkness. Those who do so are [generally] among those upon whom darkness has been inflicted. They often choose to perpetuate the pain of their existence. Once again, I say that this choice is most often *not made on a conscious level.* They mistake the joy they receive from the process (of accepting darkness) for Light. They believe that their actions bring the Light. This delusion is created by the ego and can appear to be anything that furthers the feeling of empowerment. Those who choose to live

---

[18] This is more a rejection of the Light, rather than being the choice of darkness.

under the yoke of cruelty see the darkness of it, but for most of them, that darkness is not an option; it feels like home to them. Their perception of any free choice is eventually obliterated. The darkness that one has not created on a conscious level creeps in so slowly that the individual often does not even notice the fading of the Light.

July 17, 2019

Yes, it is true that in each age of humankind, there will come to the people what they are capable of accepting [theologically and philosophically]. It may be that the general population cannot accept something right away, but the word of Truth will be picked up by at least a few. There is a period in which the seed may (or may not) take root and begin to grow. If you allow me to enhance the metaphor, the seed must be dropped upon fertile soil. It must receive the elements necessary for its growth, either by nature, general culture, or by the one selected to nurture its growth.

The seed of truth must be tended to in its cultivation by those in the environs, and word of it must be spread amongst those in the area and beyond. All of these elements are necessary, and yet even when they are present, the growing plant may still be crushed by those who do not wish it to grow for whatever reason. [They may fear the new, finding it counter to their current beliefs and too much of a threat to their carefully constructed world.]

Truth is not the defining factor in whether or not the plant takes root and grows. It is all in the nurturing, you see. For even if the seed is one of Truth and Light and all good things, if it is nurtured with soil and water that are not those which are indicated for that particular seed [used by those with ill intent], it may grow — but it will be perverted from its original intent and will not bring the Light intended with its planting. And the yield of this seed will not be good; it may even be toxic.

Yes, what I say is true for all cultures, religions, and societies, but I speak of one that has lurked in the background of these transmissions I give to you. I speak specifically of Shabbatai Tzvi. He is the example of the seed which was dropped upon the fertile soil and then was ill-nurtured. The teachings of Light and Connection with the One came to this person, who had the potential to grow and be a Light unto his people. The people sorely needed him, but the seed of potential that had been planted in him was no longer alive by the time they reached him. He had been touched early in his life by forces that were not in favor of the advent of his Light and greatness. By the time the teachings of the Light and Connection to the One reached him [and he had been looking for them], he had been ill-nurtured, and his original direction in the world had been perverted, corrupted. This is how the Truth came to be misused by him. The one who nurtured the grown plant further perverted the already misgrowing seedling. He watered it with the tainted water of ego and shone his own light upon it rather than the sun's.[19]

Our master HaAri, who saw all things and saw into the souls of each human and the future, saw exactly what would come to pass. He warned what might happen if HaAri's works were disseminated and fell into the hands of those who would pervert the Knowledge, Wisdom, and Truth of them. And indeed, it came to pass as he said it would.

---

[19] This refers to Nathan of Gaza, who considered himself the prophet (and enabler) of Shabbatai Tzvi's messianic claim.

July 17–18, 2019

And we continue. You have learned much from your research during our writings. You had studied some of it before when it was unnecessary to keep it in the forefront of your mind, and now that information has been refreshed. You have also learned new information about what we are creating together.

Yesterday, we discussed revelations concerning Shabbatai Tzvi. His example illustrates what happens when Wisdom and Knowledge are misused. The effect of such a thing occurs on so many levels, affecting so many individuals and society as a whole. Knowledge and Wisdom are then manipulated to benefit the ego of one, not the whole of society or even the few. [Here, we must also mention society's need to fulfill a certain role and the lengths they will go to suspend belief to make this situation a reality.] Yes, I am aware this situation has occurred countless times throughout history [including simultaneous occurrences at this moment in your world and time].

This example also serves to illustrate the abilities and knowledge of HaAri and others to varying degrees. His skills were honed to an extraordinary level. Even when events are foreseen, either in the form of speculation or pure and certain knowledge, certain humans, due to their specific intellectual, emotional, and spiritual needs, will suspend their beliefs and exercise their free will to allow the darkness to be spread by others. I speak of those with a strong force and the will to spread their darkness anywhere it can creep in, penetrate, and spread.

As I mentioned, there is a need for some individuals to spread their pain, and Shabbatai Tzvi suffered greatly [if privately] in his lifetime [from undiagnosed mental illness]. Those who suffer from his particular ailment[20] are at times filled with darkness [and have the unfortunate added characteristic of a strong ego]. They can be only too willing and seem to derive joy from spreading the darkness of their interiors to others. Yet Shabbatai Tzvi gave his followers hope, the hope of redemption. There are some individuals, and I may be speaking of some in the Jewish lineage [both past and future], who also suffer from the darkness, but when enough Light is present, the ego is not prevalent enough for them to succumb to it. I note some in *Sefer HaHezyanot (The Book of Visions)* who do not spread their darkness but rather reserve that pain for themselves. Instead, they spread joy to others so that others do not suffer as they do.

It should be noted that their decision to spread joy and Light adds to their supply of both. The spreading of darkness and pulling others into it may cause them and others additional pain. Such activity creates mayhem and chaos in history, much to the detriment of humanity. Does this sound familiar?

The lessons of these episodes are rarely learned — not for more than a moment in time, anyway. The dissemination of these teachings contributed to the unfortunate episode of the self-proclaimed [pseudo] messiah, Shabbatai Tzvi. Even the methods and spiritual technologies[21] developed and used in my day [not to mention in other times and places and religions and cultures] could not stem the tide of this aberrant individual and societal behavior — nor did they bring on the redemption we so desired in our time. As our master warned us, the Knowledge in the wrong

---

[20] See "Shabbatai Tzvi" in the Appendix.
[21] The work of healing with vibration, colors, permutation of the letters, combinations of words and phrases, and musical healing, et al.

hands would lead to a disastrous outcome. He did not say he knew this for sure; he made it sound as if he was speculating. Perhaps a sterner warning might have prevented the episode, but perhaps not, and the lesson was a valuable one. Of course, the learning of that lesson did not last for long [as I mentioned], later rendering the entire font of wisdom and knowledge of the Kabbalistic tradition inaccessible [and in many circles prohibited] to the greater Jewish world.

In the present time, materials and knowledge are more easily dispersed, manipulated, and distributed. There is little to no control whatsoever concerning who sees what. There is no control over the true information or the false. There is no genuine control over who has access to any or all information, and this leads to chaos when the discernment between truth and falsehood blurs.

Getting back to the case of Shabbatai Tzvi, we took precautions with the dissemination of HaAri's teachings both in our day and for the future. The plan only worked for a short time because I insisted on recording his teachings in my copious notes of what he spoke in my presence. [I could not bear for his holy words to be lost.] I also added notations and teachings that emanated from him and which I derived from what he had spoken. To those, I added knowledge and wisdom I had gained over my lifetime of learning with so many esteemed teachers.

It is said that each hears what he can hear at whatever level he is at the time of listening. And then, depending on his level, he will also interpret further from that level of understanding at which he finds himself. And so, all was not exactly as my teacher had wished. His much-stated wish was that his teachings *are not recorded for posterity* — even though he designated me as the official recorder should it happen despite his desire. [He seemed to have a clear view of the future.] Others also recorded his teachings after his death and against his wishes. They were not always true to the words I heard from him.

Please allow me to share a memory. All were not seated in the same room with HaAri [both literally and figuratively] while we learned with him. This is to say that he taught different students at different levels, in different groups (again according to their stage of learning and abilities). The groups assembled mainly at a local *beit midrash* [study hall], while some of us received our teachings in his home. We would usually sit on the floor, and, in the appropriate season, there would be a fire to warm us. I remember a sweet but somewhat spicy fragrance that could be detected in the air wherever and whenever our learning took place. The scent was meant to elevate our souls to a higher level as we sometimes learned what the earthbound aspect of our soul could not quite grasp. The incense was prepared and tended to by HaAri's wife, Rahma. She also prepared certain foods with herbs she said would be healing and nourishing. Truth be told, I can remember that scent arriving to my senses at various times throughout my life — when we no longer learned with him in his home. It would come to me while walking in a field, in a moment of intense meditation, or even in a dream. I often wondered how it could come to me without its physical presence. When I would ask Rahma about it, she would simply give me a smile of understanding.

There was a good deal of work that called for only HaAri and me to be present. Occasionally, we met in my home, which did not have nearly the same lightness and feeling of sacred space as his but was a place where we could meet without the others. At times we met in places of nothing but nature's glory. All spaces were elevated by his presence. Our meetings were not necessarily secret, but many interpreted the situation that way. Some merely envied in silence, but some exhibited jealousy that was born of their egos, which, to a degree, enslaved them and prevented their deeper understanding of the work we were doing. I say this not with ill feeling but rather to let you know that this kind of behavior exists even amongst those who consider themselves to be spiritually evolved — and this, too, has occurred throughout time.

I have diverted you from what I was discussing, but sometimes the memories of that time are most powerful and pervasive. As I spoke of the learning that went on, it was as if I were back in that time — so much so that even you could smell the aroma of the incense that burned and the sense and smell of the heavy wood furnishings that surrounded us. I could sense the rooms as if I were in them at the same moment that I spoke of them. The power of the experience was so potent that I could not let it pass without mention. You also felt and smelled and sensed the experience as a testimony to its power. The feelings that one is left with are sometimes more important than remembering the details of what was spoken. Remember that, please. I want you and all who read this to remember that.

July 21, 2019

Let us begin. You are taken with the experience that you had the other day when last we wrote, and you were able to smell the incense and then felt yourself in the room with us as we studied.

It was fleeting, but it was only a taste of what was to come for you. The ability to travel in such a fashion is not new to you, and why would you think that a person or soul who can travel to the far reaches of all creation would not be able to travel in what you call "time?" You know, after all, that time is simply a shift in consciousness. You are a master of this, and your work with us will assist you in fine-tuning your skills. It is no more than a shift of focus. In this same fashion, HaAri and others could see into the interior workings of another person, a situation, into the future, etc. It is a shift of focus that you usually are not even paying attention to because you do not have to. Others do, but you are among those who do not, and this is what some call being psychic. We would not have categorized it as such, but people like to name things.

This brings us back to our topic. I repeatedly speak of our having to work within the confines of our times, culture, and religion. We needed to have nameable pathways to the goal of *Yichud* [Unification with the One]. We needed signposts that would be recognized by those who would travel the path. One would not put out signposts on a journey in a language that would not be understood by travelers, correct? Some would intuit, but there would be many more who would not. People need instructions; people need to have the teacher speak their language [or have an interpreter].

I was, to a great extent, a sign maker and an interpreter for those with a knowledge of the journey that was much greater than mine and for those who had not yet but would make the journey. Those with the experience knew where to stop along the way, where to rest, where to eat, where to find shade, etc. Other religions also had and have those who made the journey and subsequently have written and posted signs and interpretations for those who may not understand and need further instruction. To continue the analogy: there are yet others who advertise the same basic trip, but they know different stops along the way and consider different benchmarks to give meaning to the journey. Also, the final destination may fall in a slightly different location than the "original" trip had intended or projected. Some travelers may think they have a "big" agenda but are really just meant to experience the journey differently, each in his time and each according to his own abilities and authenticity of desires. And each is guided by their Higher Self if they are able to hear and heed the guidance.

This I see more clearly now. *NO ONE is wrong*: they are simply on a different path. They are on their own journey. Not only may we have different destinations, but we may have different points of departure. We all have different levels of endurance or fear or the capacity for discomfort. This travel analogy is quite adequate for this explanation! And it is rather enjoyable as well.

There were and are many who wish not to travel at all and feel they can reach the destination by standing still — or they may feel fine right where they are and not even think of leaving their chosen position. And some actually fear both the traveler and the journey and warn the traveler not to go, and they threaten those who are the guides. This situation, too, has existed throughout your history and continues to this day. Why are some so afraid of innovation? Why do they think their way is the only way? Why must they place themselves in front of those who wish to move forward and scream "STOP?"

From my present perspective, and even from yours, we see many justifications in their minds for this. [In our time], we came upon men who found us threatening and a menace to all things they stood for. Those men were by no means evil, but they did live in fear rather than in awe and joy. The word for fear and the word for awe have the same root in Hebrew.[22] Too many live in fear when it is so much more pleasant and productive to live in awe. Whereas awe and joy free, fear controls, and fear is what is used to control the masses in every place and time. There were not masses of Jews in our part of the world, but I speak of the larger population of the Jewish people. We Kabbalists did not even have a place with many Jews, thanks to their leaders, but they came to know us through some practices, prayers, and tunes adapted to their religious world.

July 22, 2019

Let us begin today. Until now, we have focused more on the times and generalities rather than the specifics of theologies and practices we created and utilized. We have already discussed much that is meaningful and shall be expanded upon as we proceed. There is material you will need to reference so that you can help relate what I tell you coherently and understandably.

What we created in my time was complex and often heavily "coded." We saw this as a plus at the time, and it was a protection we put in place to safeguard our technologies. There is no technology that is safe if there is someone with the determination to access it. This is another thing that you already know from your

---

[22] Root word: yud-reish-aleph

time in history. Your technologies are different, your information is different, and the potential results are different, but, in principle, they are essentially the same.

The possibilities and potentials of our [spiritual] technologies were very powerful. The technologies had the potential to render a great deal of destruction should the wrong people use them for the wrong purposes. Like today, there were safeguards, but there was always someone smart enough to circumvent them. And, like today, if their genius is calling them to manipulate the technology wrongly, they cannot be stopped.

Once the technology has been exploited, its integrity has been diminished, if not destroyed. The intention has been infused into words spoken and actions performed. The basic structure has been broken, and no result that comes [from the use of it, for it has been corrupted] will ever be for good.

July 24, 2019

It is in preparation for the difficult times that the practices one has learned must be integrated and available to the mind and be called from the subconscious into the conscious. It is then that they are to be utilized and actualized for the purposes for which they were intended. It is not such a secret that none work if they are packed away and not used! It is the true master who has all these formulas, methods, and tools so internalized that they are available to them as needed. Learning these things to know them alone is equal to blasphemy. Think about the implications of that. Who would choose to learn about the tools and technologies to access both the internal and external universes [they are, in essence, the same] if they knew that not using the knowledge to make one's life and the world better is a greater *avayra* [sin] than misusing them! Think about that!

Understand what I am saying: do not step into the learning if you will not be incorporating it into your life and using the tools and technologies that are presented to you! Each has its own use. Some things are to be used daily just to improve your quality of life, your health, and the quality and health of everyone around you. Some things are to be used in times of personal or communal challenge or despair, and so on. The practices will depend on your level of sacred knowledge of both the Universe and you. Why is not using what you know a greater sin? Because to be [in this case, to learn] without purpose is counter to all reasons for coming into this world, even if your purpose is counter to the good or positive progress of the world.

It is the same as not using one's natural abilities in this world. To live in a state of fear and false humility and denial of one's natural talents is also an affront to the Source from which we emanate. It is not without reason that the gifts of each individual human being are manifested in the world. These gifts and attributes are manifested in this world because they are part of a network and a plan that is in place. This plan is for the maximum growth and evolution of humans and their world. Suppressing or withholding one's talents and gifts throws off the plan. Such is to divert the projected and intended growth and progression of the individual's life and the world around him.

Now, you must know that all the gifts given to an individual do not always appear to be positive attributes. Nevertheless, they are natural to the individual and are in place to provide growth and learning to those in the world around them and sometimes beyond. Aberrant behavior — behavior that falls outside of what society calls nurturing, positive, acceptable, or productive — is potentially also in line with the plan. Once again, I say it is not for us to judge, even though we do.

Certain individuals are given the gifts that cause [or potentially cause] mayhem and chaos, which humans think cannot possibly be God's will. But challenges must exist; else, how would man have the opportunity for growth and expansion? Overcoming chaos, mayhem, and even what you call evil is the goal of human existence. To exist in the company of Love and Light is the final goal in the end, but if you start that way, there is no room for growth. You did not have to climb the mountain or cross the ocean or struggle [make any effort — it does not need to be a struggle] in any way to arrive at the final goal. And so, the efforts of man must be employed toward that goal. Each must contribute to the "cause," whether through one's natural talents or the tools and technologies one acquires along the way. If neither is used, then there is no point in the person's life. All is dependent upon Free Will.

Remember, I spoke of intention and authenticity earlier. For some special individuals, their particular skill is to help others identify their own gifts. This ability and "service," if you will, are things that could be better employed in your society and most cultures, as many have come into this world who have no memory of nor conscious connection with their true gifts. There are indeed those who do this work in increasing numbers, but they are not always the best ones for the job.

The true essence of a soul [an individual] has often been masked by the process of coming into the body [the birth process] or through the suppression that occurs through living in a particular family or the general culture. This loss of spiritual identity does not happen so much with the more Indigenous peoples who still inhabit certain areas of the world. Generally, these Indigenous cultures honor the spirit far more than the more modern societies and have in place elders who guide spiritual life. If a person strays from their purpose/role, then they are guided [usually gently] by those in their communities who do this sort of thing. Without the input of the greater world, they are more likely to be in touch and keep aligned with their soul and purpose. No one is lost in the crowd or buried under the debris of the events and effects of the world around them.

In the various mystical traditions, the role of the teller, or reader, who sees into the soul and can report on these findings, is taken very seriously. So again, we speak of the tools and technologies that can be learned and employed and the natural guidance that follows from having learned and used these tools. Please remember that the end goal of success [in the eyes of the world] is not always achieved.

HaAri revealed to me his ability to read souls after we had established a deep relationship with each other. That is when he revealed it to me with words, but he had revealed it to me much earlier than that with his actions. It became clear as I observed him in his interactions with both his students and others whom he encountered in his life. I watched as he saw into the soul and very essence of an individual. Sometimes he chose not to reveal what he saw, but upon request, he would tell the person only part of what he saw, but not all — only what was relevant at the moment. But occasionally, he did not reveal any information, for his gift was only used with purpose.

What purpose would this skill serve if the information was kept from the individual? Do you want to know? Well, the information served in the gentle and quiet guidance that HaAri would provide in various aspects of the person's life if the individual was one who might benefit from the information [a devotee, student, a student's family, or a member of the community]. It was rarely a matter of revealing all or even most of the information but rather only that which might be helpful to a person. HaAri might use the information to help pave the way for a person in the world. It was not always [maybe even rarely] revealed to a person as a formal reading but just as a helpful observation. And the revelation of too much information might throw them off balance enough to damage their psyche.

To be honest, many did request these helpful observations from him. They asked me as well, but I deferred to him during his lifetime. This was not my calling, nor was I nearly as skilled in it at that time. Let us say it was not one of my special gifts to the world. I did not have his insight nor discernment of how much to reveal. My gift was mainly to be the student, the listener, the recorder, and in some cases, the amalgamator of thoughts and ideas of others, and then later my own. Though I was very much in awe of the gifts of my teachers, Yosef Karo, the RaMaK, HaAri, and all the others, I did not covet their gifts, nor did I ever try to adapt or claim them as my own as I saw that each has their role to play.

From an early age, I knew that I had a special role that would be revealed to me in time. I was lauded for my ability to learn, memorize, and retain the vastness of thought contained in our Torah and all the sacred texts. Yet this seemed like something other than the end game to me. From the time I was a child, it was as though I could see, or rather sense, a long road ahead of me that stretched beyond the confines of my home and my community. I saw that I would not only bring my learning to other places by virtue of my travel but that, eventually, what I knew would somehow travel to other places by some other means. I have to say that I did not understand this in the days of my youth, but the vision gave me great joy. I went with it, and then it went — without me. It gave me somewhere to escape when I needed to do that.

I was born into this world with complete faith. A human lifetime is entered into for learning and experiencing. And each one brings with them into the lifetime the essence of their soul and their outlook, as well as a purpose for this leg of the journey. For me, it was my soul's purpose to experience that particular lifetime through the lens of total faith and an unbreakable linkage to the Light and Source of all creation. And my essence, that part of me that I have carried throughout all my lifetimes, is difficulty with personal relationships and not clearly seeing what is right in front of me.

Looking back, I see this now, of course, but then it was a rather mysterious journey that I knew lay ahead of me. I saw this, as you would say in your time, like a movie in my head, right there laid out before me. It was a vision that sustained me when I felt mired in the daily learning of the texts and as I sat with my books and teachers, knowing there was more for me. In no way do I diminish our holy texts, but that kind of learning cannot be the only focus in the world of a child. It should not be. I have said several times that I learned too much too soon [intellectually] for my maturity level, and it was not helpful to my emotional development. Really, I was not very gifted in the realm of interpersonal relationships [neither as a child nor as an adult]. With the overload of knowledge coming my way, I relied on vivid visions to keep my spirit going. Not only could I see these visions in front of me, but I followed them down the path to see where they led. That information was not revealed to me by other than my mind [or perhaps my soul. Now I know that the visions were shown to me by my guides as a way to bring me hope and comfort and encouragement.]. But the sun always shone on them, and I knew that they would take me to high places eventually and that I would be happy there and come into my own. I would discover what it was to live my role in the world. My gifts would be to listen, learn, and teach. I did not know exactly how I would teach in the world of these masters, who were true lights unto the world, but I had faith that all would be revealed to me at the perfect time.

July 29, 2019

And indeed, the revelations did come to pass, as I was well positioned for what was to be my destiny, development, and role in the world. I now see a web [of connection] of sorts in the structure of the Universe from the largest aspects of Creation to the smallest. Right now, I will refer to the design of connections that existed in my time and world, and perhaps you will see the similarities as they may apply to your life and your world. There are connections that we make in life on many different levels.

There are some forces that inform us of what is and what is to come. Sometimes, we recognize this information either in part or fully formed, and sometimes not at all. Information is given to us as we can hear it and in a way that we [individually and communally] can assimilate it. How we make use of the information is completely up to us. [Again, Free Will.] We must be aware and recognize the markers along the way if we want to maximize our impact in this world. This was a major occupation of the Kabbalists of my day [and other times, of course, but I wish to speak only of my lifetime and experience]. It is as though some humans in the world have their receiving devices so finely tuned that they seem to miss no sign or marker along the way, while the rest of us simply do our best to see all that we can and make the connections whenever possible.

═══◆═══

From the Transcriber
Some sixty years after HaAri's death, Rabbi Yaakov Tzemach described R. Hayyim's initiation into the Arizal's new approach to Kabbalah:

> 'When I, Rabbi Chaim Vital, came to my teacher of blessed memory [the Arizal] to study this [Kabbalistic] wisdom, my teacher of blessed memory went to Tiberias and took me with him... and when we were on a boat in the water, opposite the pillars of the old synagogue, my teacher of blessed memory then took a cup and filled it with water from between the pillars, and gave me that water to drink, and said to me: Now you will attain with this that wisdom, for

this water that you have drunk is from Miriam's well. And from then on, I began entering the depths of this wisdom.'²³

R. Hayyim elaborated on HaAri's effect on him in today's discussion with me.

———◆———

At that moment in this story, I felt lifted by his wings, and we ascended to heights I could never have known on my own. As if only the combination of our two souls together could have achieved this ascent to the upper world[s] that I had not previously experienced. It was in those places [for there was not just one] that miracles could be worked, new worlds and understandings could be seen, and the work that needs to be done in our world could be more efficiently accomplished. Even after he was no longer in this world, that day and the memory of combining our soul energy and force propelled me forward in the continuation of the work we had begun together.

To be truthful, once I passed through the depth of my initial grief at his passing, I realized that he would be forever with me.²⁴ We would continue our work as before but with an adjustment to the lack of his physical presence. The sensation of that very moment was the calling point for my soul from that moment on.

---

²³ "The Healing Water from the Well of Miriam," *Temple of Miriam the Prophetess*, accessed December 25, 2022, https://templeofmiriam.com.
²⁴ In his spiritual autobiography, *Sefer HaHezyanot (The Book of Visions)*, R. Hayyim refers several times to feeling abandoned by his beloved master. Those who advised him (from other realms) explained that these feelings came at times he was neither living according to his purpose nor doing the things he was meant to do.

It was the feeling to which I aspired and for which I longed. It was indeed the feeling that carried me through the rest of my days.

July 30, 2019

From the Transcriber
What R. Hayyim shared with me yesterday was beautiful — like a song. I thanked him for his words and the feeling behind them.

———◆———

Many think that we were solely intellectual in our pursuits, and one would, of course, think that given the amount of material HaAri and I learned and taught during our time on Earth. We were able to commit huge volumes of material to memory, and from that, combined with our intuition and the oral teachings that were passed on to us through our tradition's necessary teachers, we created what appeared to be new pathways and technologies to align ourselves with the Source of Creation. [It is to say that we did not create the pathways but rather revealed them.] Beyond that, we were men of great depth of feeling that was not expressed nor experienced in the ways of most humans we knew.

Our passions and desires were channeled into our flights toward Unification with the One and into our healing and other work that we did on the deepest level of the soul. For me, it was always the deepest connection on the soul level that aroused the feelings in my heart and lifted me as nothing else could. For all the words I'd used in my life, and they were many, I valued the most that for which I had no words. And once I began my all too brief time on Earth[25] with my master teacher and partner in the mysteries, HaAri, Rabbi Yitzchak ben Solomon Luria, I would never be the same. Throughout my many long years in Safed, and they felt very long to me then, I sometimes suffered as much and equal to the heights that I soared. I now know it was, but in the blink of an eye — maybe two blinks in my case since I lived for many years. For all the intellectual splendor I experienced with my other brilliant teachers, nothing lit the fire of my soul as did my journeys with him.

There are souls with whom we are fortunate enough to connect that ignite the intense fire we remember from when we existed only in the form of spiritual energy. They have the honor of giving us the gift of rekindling the flame of recognition and connection to the One. Not everyone is so fortunate to have a kindred soul come to perform this rekindling. And not everyone recognizes if and when it happens. That is not to say that an event, a memory, or some other form of recognition cannot accomplish the same end. But when a kindred soul performs this mission for us, not only does the flame of recognition get rekindled, but the love with which it is performed brings the experience to another level in degrees of Love and awareness of our holy nature. This is a love that few understand as it is not a physical love, though it can, at times, be mistaken for such a thing. Unlike the physical aspects of love, this one does not fade nor diminish with time or experience.

Here I must explain something related to what I just said. There are times that a kindred soul will appear in physical form

---

[25] R. Hayyim lived to age 86.

during our lifetime to remind us of something — perhaps a mission that we came here to accomplish, for example, or a lesson that we need to learn or to remember who we really are — and then that soul, in human form, may fade from our life with us, whether by death or estrangement. [The connection may be fleeting in nature and does not necessarily connote a relationship.] Once their mission is accomplished, they no longer need to stay present in our life. They may or may not remain a part of our life. These very deep soul relationships can serve their purpose quickly or stay for a lifetime. This is a large subject, and we will take it up later, but it was worth mentioning at this point.

As HaAri helped me in life, he also remained my companion after his death. He did not disappear from my life or my world. He guided my hand as I wrote his words. [Else, how could I have recalled with such exactitude the details as well as the breadth of his teachings?] He directed me to a multitude of experiences throughout the rest of my life and continued to accompany me on flights to the other realms to maintain and continue to advance the healing and spiritual repair work that we did during his lifetime. He took me once to the secluded place on the river Nile[26] where he first encountered Elijah, our Prophet, during the times of his seclusion and initial study of the Zohar, our core mystical text. We traveled together in spirit not only to places on this Earth but to places in the Universe that one could never imagine within the confines of the human mind.

———◆———

[26] He lived in Cairo from age eight until 36.

From the Transcriber

R. Hayyim now reminds me of a method of repair and Light healing I did a couple of years ago. I never knew where this technique originated and certainly not how it came into my mind and practice, but he tells me, "Yes, of course, I directed you to it, as it was a practice of mine." He also tells me we can renew this particular method and refine the process. This serves as an example of a few different things. 1) We are always guided. 2) We are to go with the guidance as long as it has positive feelings of love attached to it. 3) Sometimes, we do the work even when we do not realize it. I was under the impression that I was not doing his work because I was not actively writing this book. I was wrong.

At this point in his narrative, Reb Hayyim addressed me specifically:

> 'Do you think I would choose someone for this work who did not have the gift of sight themselves? How could that be? You will drink with me of the cup of Knowledge, and we, too, shall fly to the heights from which you can see even more than you do at this time. We too will work with the combination of our soul forces to heal and repair and redeem in the world in which you live as well as worlds beyond.'

———◆———

HaAri and I would greet each morning as if it were the first we had ever witnessed. We would savor each morning just in case it was to be the last. And so, it is to begin a day in love and awe of all there is, of all Creation. Such is a day begun in Love and Light, and Love of Light. It was this Love we not only absorbed but wore as both our inner and outer garments so that we might remind ourselves and others of the Love and Light in the world. We hoped that this would direct the thoughts of others to that goal as well. His was not worn on his body but was rather the entirety of him. Yet for me, it was but a cloak, as I was sure that on the inside, there was something that I could not overcome in myself to be the pure Light that he was.[27]

This was a step toward redemption, for as one lives in and emanates the Light, it spreads and flows wherever one steps, like a carpet. It leaves a path for others on which they will hopefully choose to tread. This is how some of the most powerful spiritual work of all is accomplished. To absorb and amplify the Light that is cast upon us is the work we are all here to do [in all times and all places]. There are at least as many interpretations of how to do this as there are humans and other sentient creatures on the planet. [It is just that the humans are the ones who intellectualize this, and it is they whom I address.] All the rest of what we do to achieve the goal are but ruffles and flourishes in the process. Different cultures and religions add their particular processes and technologies to the mix. In the end, it is all about receiving the energies of Love and Light and transmitting them into the world [and the Universe] at the highest level possible. [Modulation is sometimes necessary.]

---

[27] Added May 8, 2022.

July 31, 2019

From the Transcriber

It seems that R. Hayyim rather likes it when I read what others have written so that he can use it as a taking-off point for his commentary. He directs me to particular sites and materials dealing with things he wishes to speak about. Unfortunately, he usually begins his commentary before I have finished reading even one paragraph.

———✦———

There were indeed major shifts in theology and practice in my day. We went from how much you know to where you can spiritually travel [with what you know]. Where can *you go* with what you know? And is the knowing enough? Indeed, we came to believe that the knowledge [of texts, ritual, and practice] was no longer the singular driving force and the power behind our Judaism [besides faith in the Almighty Source of All]. We came to believe [initially, just those in our circle] that our lives must not be solely based on strict adherence to the laws. We needed to incorporate certain esoteric practices (not merely those of the already prescribed rituals) to instill the elevation and joy in serving God and unifying with the One, the Source of All, whom we referred to as God. Through this service, we would assist in uplifting humanity and travel along a path to personal and communal redemption.

For me, it was as if I came out from within the pages of the books [as though I had been trapped inside those very pages], and I lifted myself out of those pages and grew wings. I took the knowledge and seasoned it with my intuition and guidance. As I released that which was not relevant to this earthly journey, I rose higher and higher — first out of the book, then above the room, the building, and the town, and then up and up and up. I was able to see the true reality more clearly the further I was away from what I had known as reality. When I took flight, I was free in a way that I could not be free while holding on to all the worldly knowledge that had anchored me previously.[28] It was as if the rules that had served as an anchor for me and society on Earth were no more than self-imposed chains and weights as I saw them from above. Somehow, they still seemed necessary when in the earthly realm, but as I took flight, the links [of the chain] dropped away one by one, as none of them would have allowed for this journey. I was eventually able to be fully present in each of the worlds I passed through simultaneously, for being fully present is what moves us forward. **This is something very important to remember.**

Although most others did not know quite the extent of the heights that I was able to reach, it was apparent to many that I had achieved a lightness and a Light that had not previously been seen in me.[29] People often wish to partake in this, to achieve this, or to at least touch one who has. HaAri sent forth a Light unto the world and its people from which no one could hide. He created liturgy and practices that people easily took upon themselves and adapted [in various iterations] through time until this day.

---

[28] For in those higher realms, none of the book learning was of any consequence.
[29] This lasted in me for the duration of my time with HaAri, but only intermittently after his passing.

Hidden within those practices, he infused elements of Light and [what some may call] magic. He embedded a vibrational seed in all, designed to awaken, release, and intensify the Light in both the person and the soul, performing the practice, reciting words, or resonating with a tune. When I use the word magic, I mean to say that his personal creation of the word, practice, thought, or song placed in it a spark of Light and Life. No one knew (or realized) how he could achieve such a thing, and yet he did. And so, the Light of whatever he knew and whatever he brought to the world was carried on to this day and for all time. All who knew him glowed in his presence and those who wished to continue this glow gathered in his circle. By creating these other vehicles for the Light, he was able to widen the circle and increase the spread of the Light and, hence, the chances for Redemption. If you can understand, this was a way of elevating us all so that we might bring on what we saw as the sorely needed Messianic Age through our mass efforts. For HaAri, not only was this desired result important to him, but his fellow humans also chose to participate for the pure joy it brought them. It seemed as if he knew how far and wide and into the future this would be perpetuated.

In the creation of such liturgy, rituals, and practices, we were guided by spirits who had ascended and wished, from their heavenly positions, to assist us in achieving holiness within ourselves and bringing it into the world. We were guided in our studies, in our meditations, and in our everyday lives. I use the word "heavenly" in its generic sense and would not necessarily use that word to provide a more advanced understanding of the concept. These spirits, or energies which were our teachers, came to us in different ways — some through meditation, some through the dream state and prayer, each in its own way. HaAri had our Prophet Elijah; Yosef Karo had his Maggid.[30] Some of us came by these visitations naturally and without conscious effort, but some of us developed and used techniques of Unification with our Source of Being, and in the pursuit of this, on the journey, we would receive the messages and the guidance we yearned for. Here again, we created these travel guides and road maps to take us on the divine journeys. Some needed them, and some did not. And some took wrong turns even with the map in front of them.

It was through these teachers who came to us in our various states of consciousness that we were infused with the sparks of Light that we, in turn, infused into the world through the different methods I earlier described [as well as just by our presence]. The input levels of these non-physical teachers varied, depending on their strength and the vessels for their knowledge, who were usually members of our circle of influence. I will discuss this system [yes, I will call it a system — of transference] as a separate issue and in its place. People like to hear about this sort of thing, and many would like to partake in it. I will discuss it, as I said, in its own time and place. This is amusing since it is the very essence of what we are doing at this moment to create the work on these very pages.

Related to this, to some degree, is what the author you read discussed about our community in Safed being close to the *kevers* [gravesites] of our holy teachers who had passed on to the higher realms. What he [the author] says about the *kevers*, or the burial sites of the great mystics, was true for us. At the time, we felt we

---

[30] See "The Maggid of Joseph Karo" in the Appendix.

could contact them through our proximity to them. But as you are personally experiencing, physical proximity to a physical marker of any kind has nothing to do with facility of contact with the soul. But in our time, and to some in your time and throughout time, it provides an anchor, focus, and great solace.[31]

———◆———

What came into your mind when reading is that our time was one of an inner exploration of God, as opposed to previously held notions of God as other — I will explain your vision. There were so many different ways to approach the path to Unification, and what you just now saw in your mind was one of them.

As if launched into space and time (knowing that those are all the same anywhere and everywhere) but as a frame of reference for those who find themselves in that belief — this is where there exists a greater density of God [Source] energy. This particular journey of yours was brief because the penetration into that energy was so deep as to not be sustainable. It was not one from which any lucid information was derived but rather the experience of an intimate and profound penetration into the highest concentration of the Creative Force. Although your vision was humorous to you, it was the best vision I could give you.

———◆———

---

[31] For some fascinating details about beliefs surrounding grave visitation in general (Jewishly speaking) and specifically about R. Isaac Luria and R. Menachem Mendel Shneerson, see Morris Faierstein, "Grave Visitation by Rabbi Isaac Luria and Rabbi Menachem Mendel Schneerson," *Modern Judaism* 36, no. 1 (2016): pp. 31-41.

From the Transcriber

I experienced a vision of a human-like being (me) being launched straight up at an incredible velocity, and it came closer and closer to the vicinity of a yellow orb. And as it approached closer and closer, I suddenly made contact with the orb — it had the elasticity of a balloon — I seemed to enter into it but was just pushed in as far as the material of the orb would stretch, and then I was shot right back out and back — back to where I came from. As with a balloon, the human missile [for lack of a better word] went in as far as it could without breaking it, and the force of the balloon's resistance shot it back out. So, there was no penetration of the actual interior of the balloon. But that was probably as close as one could get without breaking the balloon. Aha! Ultimate penetration would break the balloon and the interior of the Creative Force. The Source of All can indeed never completely be experienced by its creations!

MYSTICAL AUTHENTICITY

August 2, 2019

In the cave where he dwelled for 13 years, Shimon bar Yochai[32] did not learn text, for the text came later and stemmed from his experiential learning of the mysteries during his years of confinement [which was not the usual order of things]. His education was experiential, and that was the essence of his teaching to those who would follow him. But as with all mystical teachings [at one time or another], the mysteries became more hidden and awaited their "waking" until the right moment in time and until the right one for the job of discovering and working with the mysteries appeared. This is why many of those mysteries were revealed to us in our time. It was the right time, the right place, and the right "players were in the game." Some of the mystery teachings were passed down orally, and some through text — while remaining hidden in plain sight, and some of the deepest and most beautiful teachings of the mysteries came down through

---

[32] Shimon bar Yochai was a second century Rabbi of high regard and standing who studied with the great Rabbi Akiva and later went on to become the initiator (in that time, of Kabbalah — the received mysteries). Because of his antagonism toward the Romans, he, and his son Eleazar were forced to take refuge in a cave — for 13 years. It was the learning and later the teachings that came from that time that the Kabbalists attribute to the Zohar, the central and sacred Kabbalistic text to this day.

history in the form of symbols. And within all those mysteries were even more layers of hidden teachings.

Visual symbols have always been and continue to be an exquisite way of communicating both the ordinary and the mysterious in this physical world since the beginning of history. Layers of meaning and understanding are revealed to those capable of understanding, but only when they are open to it. Just as with text and oral teachings, it is the same with understanding symbols. The symbols represent thoughts and ideas, and the representation of them communicates from one to another [the recipient of which is tuned into them] the desired message that is important to the soul of the one who sees and recognizes it. There were and are both subtle and less-than-subtle manifestations of these symbols in the world. Where one person sees just a pretty visual, another will be struck with fascination and begin to penetrate the meaning that lies beneath the visual: pieces of art, furnishings, fabric designs, clothing, architectural representations, even what we think of as games — I refer specifically to what you call cards (playing cards, Tarot cards, etc.) — and so on. There are general meanings to the symbols, and there are those special meanings that their creator infused into them and those that the intuition of the viewer leads them to discover.

As symbols were embedded so long ago for those of every generation to discover, it was thus that HaAri implanted meaning and symbols to manifest the sparks of Light that he embedded in the prayers and meditations that he created. It was through the symbols and their vibrations that the initial composers of the Kabbalistic thought and texts embedded within them that HaAri had his deepest knowing awakened during his time of seclusion[33] and exclusive study of those texts. They are what helped to awaken and magnify the Light within him that had not been previously revealed and also brought to him the Prophet Elijah to guide him for the rest of his days. The symbols of ours and other traditions persist because when the written word is not permitted to be disseminated or used publicly, the symbols will survive to tell the stories that would otherwise not live on. [This process also takes place with the use of tonal or vibrational triggers that occur within the music.]

I also want to speak today of the turning point that occurred during our era. The text of Jewish life was our nourishment, our food, our sunlight, and our water. Those who came just before me (and some who lived during my time but were older and more learned than I) built a structure for the Jewish world with their accumulated knowledge and incredible minds. They created a superior structure of our laws, rules, and Wisdom that categorized all. With the enormity of their work, both the general and dispersed population of the Jewish people could have a reference guide on which to base their observances and behaviors. This would be where their myriad of life questions could be answered. Yosef Karo and his huge work, *Beit Yosef*, with a more

---

[33] Luria had spent approximately six years in almost total isolation on an island in the Nile. He took that time to study a copy of the Zohar that he obtained. There on the island, he studied the text with the prophet Elijah as his guide.

to-the-point version called the *Shulchan Aruch*[34] [*Set or Prepared Table*], which lays out into specific categories the laws and customs and rulings on them that order the behavior and observances of the Jewish people. And Moses Cordovero, my beloved teacher whose *Pardes Rimonim* [*Garden of the Pomegranates*][35] categorized the ideas of Kabbalah and its history into a central source of information — for this had never been done before in this way.

I have mentioned before how each of us has a gift to offer, and each offered in the time and place for it to be received and by the one who can present it like no other. These two men are a perfect example of this. They gave us two structured works that covered both the everyday practical world and the philosophy and thought of the received mystical traditions of Kabbalah, the practical and the spiritual. They provided a structure and solid base in the Jewish world for what was coming next and coming quickly. In almost no time at all, a transition was made from these two solid foundations of Jewish life, compiled by well-respected scions of the Jewish world, to an uplifted and intoxicating interpretation of

---

[34] "The Shulchan Arukh ('Set Table') is the most widely accepted code of Jewish law ever written. Compiled in the 16th century by Rabbi Joseph Karo, it is a condensed and simplified version of the Beit Yosef, a commentary that Karo wrote on the Tur. Karo's rulings are in accordance with Sephardic traditions; the text of the Shulchan Arukh also includes the glosses of Rabbi Moshe Isserles, which cite Ashkenazic traditions."
"About Shulchan Arukh," *Sefaria*, accessed January 20, 2023, https://www.sefaria.org/Shulchan_Arukh,_Even_HaEzer?tab=contents.

[35] The pomegranate is an ancient symbol in the Jewish tradition. It relates to the mitzvot by the number of seeds being matched to the number of mitzvot (613). Also, it was one of the seven species in the Torah, it is said to be the forbidden fruit of the Tree of Life in the Garden of Eden, and it is the basis for the sefirot — the emanations through which all creation flows in the Kabbalistic Tree of Life.

both the Kabbalistic traditions and the practical nature of our laws and codes. These illustrious teachers who composed the volumes that I mentioned [in addition to many other scholarly works they wrote] were integral participants in the transitional energies that were to bring about the shift. In the way that our practices moved into the more experiential nature of the teachings of Kabbalah, these men had already done so in their ways. Their scholarly status gave them a tremendous level of gravitas that also lent itself to assist in the transition to the more experiential aspects of spirituality.

Yosef Karo indeed had his Maggid, his spiritual teacher from another realm, much in the way I speak to you, though his process was infinitely more dramatic. The Maggid of Yosef Karo spoke to him of practical matters as well as his behavior. The Maggid was said by some to be the embodiment of the Mishnah.[36] Through the teachings of this Maggid, we, the next generation, and Moses Cordovero benefited greatly. It was due to the man whom Yosef Karo was, along with his piety and service to the One, that the Maggid came to him and, through his guidance, brought to my beloved community in Safed. The Maggid knew what was ahead for us and of the imminent shift in our understandings and traditions. Yosef Karo decided to participate in the plan, even though he was not necessarily made aware of it on a conscious level. He knew the holiness of the voice that had come to guide him, and he chose to participate in a plan that was as yet [possibly]

---

[36] The Mishnah is the first major written collection of the Jewish oral traditions (the Oral Torah) and the first major work of Rabbinic literature. In the beginning of the third century, the Mishnah was redacted by Judah ha-Nasi.

unbeknownst to him. And so, we have both the Maggid and Josef Karo to thank for what was to unfold in Safed. So it is with the voices that come to us: they generally have [or know of] a much better plan for us than we could ever conceive.

You read of those who dispel the authenticity or reality of the energies who come to speak with those in this material world of formation. Too many people have been robbed of the ability to extend themselves or accept that which comes from beyond a place that they have experienced with their five senses. For many, many years, the mainstream world of Judaism, and, in fact, the mainstream world of the general culture, has been more than discouraged from accepting that which is beyond the five senses and what has been previously written and accepted as common knowledge.[37]

There was, as you know, a very directed effort by some, not too many [just a couple of] centuries ago, to obliterate the joy and beauty that our mystical Kabbalistic knowledge and practices gave rise. These are the people who will discredit the validity of the source of the transmissions that came to us. It is those who are, as you say, on the edge of new technologies, whether they be scientific or spiritual, who are often thought to be quite mad. The masses [as well as those in control] take their compliant passivity and stringency as the accepted way to conduct a life. As for those with passion and daring — well, they are not to be tolerated since

---

[37] In the eighteenth and nineteenth centuries there was an active effort to quiet any connection to the mystical aspects of Judaism, including the opposition to Hasidism by Europe's Mitnagdim, and later the leaning toward a Wissenschaft approach to Judaism. Wissenschaft is the "science of Judaism," or the critical approach to Jewish Studies.

they have the potential to cause much strife in the world and upset the accepted way of things. However, usually, this sort of situation historically runs in cycles, as you may have noted.

In our day and our world, few dared to doubt the sanity of a scholar who could produce works of Yosef Karo's caliber. Indeed, I bore witness to the Maggid's speech that occurred regularly and was personally privy to his revelations on those occasions. And indeed, the Maggid brought us a foreshadowing of the changes that were about to come to pass. The combination of such a revered *halachist* [specialist in laws and practices] and a man with mystical connections served quite literally as a bridge from one age to another. Another foreshadowing was that many of the things put forth by the Maggid, through Yosef Karo, evolved into some of what was put forth in the work of our teacher Moses Cordovero, the RaMaK.

What was unique about the Maggid of Yosef Karo was that it ensconced itself in the identity of a body of work, the Mishnah. Rather than presenting as a personality or a previously incarnated personage, as it was with the other guidance that came to us, the Maggid presented as a compendium of Knowledge — and this was most unique. Perhaps it was because of the caliber of Yosef Karo that the energy presented itself in this way.

Each individual has a range of what they can accept into their consciousness. For example, if you [the transcriber] had never studied our era, the work we did, or the people who lived, you may not have been able to accept me into your consciousness. Those who are to receive the work being put forth into the world are carefully chosen for fairly obvious reasons. We are not always flawless in our decisions due to free will and human variables. On occasion, the efforts at contact are futile, but we do "vet" those we choose to receive the information.

REPAIRING THE WORLD

August 12, 2019

From the Transcriber
R. Hayyim, you always direct me to read something to spark your topic of the day. Several things I read within the same half-page made me take notice and open my eyes wide. I received more information than I knew about Tikkun, Gilgul, messianism, and YOU! Can we discuss these things in print, please? I heard your very loud denials when I read a particular piece about you. But let us deal with the things in order of their appearance, please, even though I am anxious to get to the last part first.

Is your intention in this work to correct what you wrote in your original works or to change your reputation (meaning the misperceptions about you, your motivations, your work, and your character)?

═══◆═══

Now you understand, and you can hear that I am happy to have you arrive at this point of information. You have, in your current world, something called "spin." This is not new in any way other than the name. There has been a spin on all aspects of Kabbalah [and Kabbalists] throughout time by those who do not wish the general public to come in contact with the Truth. Not that all who profess to be Kabbalists are Truth speakers. There are, however, those with integrity who follow the word for the sake of the Divine [*b'shem hashamayim* – for the sake of heaven] and not for the self. They, indeed, are the Truth speakers. The message of the divinely received word is powerful beyond what most men will ever know. Countering this, there are always those who wish the world to have less Light than more. They generate and perpetuate a negative spin on the topic, the practitioners and followers of the mysteries, the Truth, and the Light. Inevitably, through the ages, since voices that speak Truth cannot be quieted [for long], they must be discredited. Instead of the extreme measure of complete censure, which can sometimes backfire, stories can discredit or redirect the praise and reputation to areas that are more acceptable to the mainstream. [Once again, you see by the examples of this in your day some things do not change.]

The liturgy, *kavannot* [directed intention, focus], and practices of HaAri have been widely accepted over time, but not necessarily with his intent, depth, and meaning. Through general usage and adaptation, much of the "magic" and sparks of Light they contain have been extremely diluted. There are certain individuals who do and always will connect with the original, but they are few and far between. This is how the world has always operated.

I am at the same time lauded, discredited, and misrepresented in our history. Perhaps I wish to correct all that you mentioned as my objective in addition to what I originally proposed to you. My original motive and proposal to you were to revise some of my work from the new perspective I have gained from a distance in time and space. This is neither restricted to human form nor place and time; for those who study the word, the deed, the history, and flow, truth should be injected to reveal the way things actually happened. This can make a difference to those who wish to know the truth of a culture, a time, or a flow of knowledge. As with the flow of a river that, over time, slowly bends and turns through forces of nature, I wish to correct the flow of the river of Truth to its original course. It is for this reason that I tell you that I was not merely the recording secretary for our master teacher HaAri HaKadosh, as many thought. Still, I was, in my own right, a teacher and creator of many philosophies and theologies, and a writer of copious amounts of works of great depth and thought.

I did consider myself to be the keeper of the gate to all teachings of HaAri [and I was, in fact, called upon to do so by him] and the guardian of his good name and practices. I did not consider myself his successor or the usurper of his "throne." Know this: neither he nor I, at any time in our lives, had messianic aspirations. There were those amongst his followers who believed in the possibility of his being the messiah, especially given his close association with the Prophet Elijah and our deep desire to bring about the Messianic Age and the redemption of our people. But he never purported to be anything of the sort. Any implication that he considered himself in the category of messiah comes especially from those who wished us ill as well as those who did not understand him or me. And sometimes they were one and the same, at once exalted and vilified. When people of any time do this, it is either malicious or ignorant, but when perpetuated throughout hundreds of years, it is out of fear — fear that the Truth will be recognized and listened to. Sometimes, the misinformation is obvious, and sometimes, it is just enough to plant a seed of doubt that will grow with proper attention.

Our work, as I have mentioned several times previously, was specifically directed toward the redemption of the Jewish people, the world in general, and bringing on the Messianic Age which would precipitate that redemption. That was a far cry from believing ourselves to be the messiah. Just as in today's world, you see that technology creates with good intentions (for the most part) and, indeed, is used for those intentions. That very same technology can also be used for the most deviant and diabolical purposes. We used our work as it was intended [to reclaim the sparks of Light and redeem the world and ourselves], but our work was then used for the ill-intended purposes of a deviant mind. Shabbatai Tzvi fed off our well-intentioned work and through his efforts, our work became tainted. He had no real understanding of anything beyond the demands of his ego [and his madness] and would use anything to achieve its goals. I have cleared the air of these facts now and given some explanation and having done so, I conclude the matter.

So, you want to discuss HaAri's theories of *Tikkun*.[38] As you know, his theories were based on what was written about in the Zohar, and often it might have been something that was merely mentioned in the text and not expounded upon. However, it was brought to his attention through his own studies, whether by his findings or with the help and direction of his guide, our Prophet Elijah.

---

[38] *Tikkun* (Repair) – In this document, refers to the processes by which restoration of the Light (that had scattered due to the breaking of the vessels in which it had been contained) and repair (of the broken vessels) were to be accomplished.

The idea of *Tikkun* moved from concept into the realm of actual doing. Mankind was to be an active participant in the redemption. By the rescue and return of the sparks of Light to God, the world would be repaired with each intentional action. This was the innovation that came through HaAri's spirit. [The actual repair of the cosmic web could be achieved "as above, so below" and vice versa, as you say.] How can we repair God if God is perfect, you ask? Flaws appear as we are flawed. As we strive for [and act with the intention of] the perfection of ourselves, we repair the flaws that we perceive in God that were created by His creations — us.

The correct performance of the commandments requires the proper intention, and Luria composed special prayers toward this end called *kavvanot* [intentions]. These *kavvanot* were an integral part of the process of *Tikkun* and gave us a hint of the dimension of praxis that accompanied Lurianic theory. The role of man in redeeming the sparks has a certain magical quality about it, and this is particularly evident in the doctrines of Luria's disciple Hayyim Vital: by action within this world, man can affect God. However, earlier Jewish mysticism had posited a distinct relationship between man's actions and God. [Man was seen as a microcosm of God]. Luria gave this notion a central position in his Kabbalah. If Jewish mysticism was never purely contemplative, it became downright active with Luria. Once one has read Luria, it becomes impossible to hold that mysticism must necessarily lead to passivity.[39]

---

[39] Paul E. Szarmach, ed., "Jewish Mysticism in the Sixteenth Century," *Medieval Mystics*, 129–202, Albany, New York: State University of New York Press, 1984.

August 13, 2019

We will continue from where we left off yesterday. I spoke of *Tikkun*, the actions we can take to repair the world. This is a favored concept in your modern Jewish world. *Tikkun Olam* [repair of the world] is what brings and then holds many Jews into the fold of their religion, rather than religious observances that are more traditional. It is not exactly how we conceived of *Tikkun*, but it is based upon our concepts, and it is valid. [Indeed, the concept has evolved over time, as all things do.] All positive action is valid in the efforts to reclaim the sparks of Light that are scattered and dispersed throughout the world. All actions that speak to the higher aspects of man's humanity, the Light within him, and the Holy Spirit are actions toward the holy end. The holy end is the redemption of the human spirit and steps closer to the reunification of that spirit with its creator, the Source of All. By performing these acts of repair, we essentially clear and clean the pathways for the Divine Light to flow into creation. This has to do with the flow of Light and energy from the Divine through the spheres of emanation, the Sefirot.[40]

It is the duty of each incarnated soul to assist in redeeming the sparks of Light scattered upon the Earth, to draw them out, and to bring them to a place where they become visible to the individual and other souls. In this way, the sparks of Light can be delivered to Source itself. In our time, we believed that each soul

---

[40] Sefirot are the emanations, the 10 attributes/emanations/channels in Kabbalah, through which the Holy of Holies – The *Ein Sof*, the One Without End makes Itself known. Through these 10 channels, the Light of the Holy One passes to create all that exists in both the physical realm and all other realms as well. See "The Kabbalistic Tree of Life" in the Appendix.

had a quota of sparks to redeem while in human form and that the return to this world, *gilgul* [reincarnation], was in part to fulfill this quota, which was not limited to one lifetime. Of course, the topic of *gilgul* was much more complicated, but this is where it connects with *Tikkun*. We will hopefully deal in depth with *gilgul* in its own section.

Many things that I mention are more complex than one can convey by merely mentioning them. My main point in these transmissions is to illuminate Truths and relate them to your world. I wish to show them to be relevant to your time and to point out that some things are timeless and in the loop of circumstance, experience, and repeated actions until something changes to break the loop. What needs to be dealt with in more depth will appear in specialized segments devoted to those specific topics. Things have not developed as either of us believed that they would in this work, but they have developed as they need to.

======◆======

Perhaps I am not quite finished with one of the topics from yesterday — well, a branch of the topic anyway. Many of the concepts, theories, and ideas that we put forward were so greatly diminished, if not outright undone, by those who were not of a state of being that could fully comprehend the material. This, too, is something that has occurred throughout the history of humans. They understood enough to recognize innovation, they knew enough to recognize something different and powerful, and their egos wanted to claim it for their own. And if they could not, they wanted to discredit or destroy it. Was the pure and unadulterated

Truth of HaAri's and my ideas and innovations unavailable to these men? Their versions were watered down because this was necessary. Because of their egos and motives, the real Truth could not be made available to them, and they could not have understood it as intended anyway.

To begin with, the information and documents that had been obtained from me were stolen for all practical purposes. One copyist would begin the adulteration, and so it continued forward down the line. Also, some could only believe and put forward the version they heard or otherwise perceived because of their own limitations. The full Truth could not be revealed to them, though they purported to desire it desperately [and they also claimed to have it]. Or perhaps they were satisfied to put forth something, anything, just to put themselves in the public eye. Truth was never their goal, even if they deluded themselves into thinking it was. Unfortunately, their teachings were also disseminated.

To be honest, I am not sure which is more dangerous to the general population — the unadulterated Truth or the material that the pretenders put forth. This is familiar to your age as it is in all ages. There are those who claim to have the Knowledge of the great and true luminaries. They claim connections that cannot be corroborated, and some are just satisfied to be connected with those who claim to be connected. It is always amazing that, throughout time, there are those who believe that their falsehoods will never be discovered. They think they will stand tall on a pile that we know will crumble with the force of one breath. You see evidence now in your day as well, and it has always been this way. It is not my duty nor desire to put names to those I am referring to but to point out that it occurred in our day and especially in the century that followed. Although there were reports of HaAri and me that were from direct witnesses, those stories were no doubt embellished, and with the effects of both time and distance from the original sources, the less likely the accuracy of the stories.

August 15, 2019

From the Transcriber

Today R. Hayyim noted the importance of my studying but was concerned it would overwhelm me. He reminded me that our work was holy, so my focus needed to be holy. "My preferred method would be to release the mind from the physical world in which you find yourself," he told me. "But when one is in public, as you are, it is not easy and sometimes undesirable. Perhaps you should know that the distractions of the outside world are more often than not distractions that you create for yourself."

HOLY TIME AND SPACE: THE SABBATH

August 17, 2019

From the Transcriber
Sometimes it is so difficult to pay attention with so many physical distractions. Can you address this issue of the flies, please, and make them go away?

———◆———

You are amusing when you think I can do anything. Just release the flies from your consciousness. You will see. [I did, and they did!]

So today, we will discuss holy time and space and their need. It is necessary to set aside time and space filled with holiness and devoid of the chaos with which the world and our lives are filled [more so in your day than in mine]. The need is universal, and the results that can come from more human participation in this particular observance of time have been set aside. For some, the observance is marked by a day, a particular set time in the calendar in the schedule of daily life. This is good as a reminder to most to stop and take time out. The day regularly comes like Shabbat [the Sabbath], which is comforting and likely to be observed. Shabbat comes with rules and regulations that have grown in scope throughout time, so strict observance of the rules keeps many from observing the intention of the day.

In your world, observance of the rules is made most difficult by the surrounding culture. Even if one lives in an area conducive to observance, the rules are still difficult and daunting to the uninitiated. Initially, one can lose the meaning of the day in the copious number of rules to be followed. Perhaps just keeping in mind the basic tenets "Do not create" and Do not destroy" can be enough to start. This is a world in which we need not improve ourselves or anyone or anything else. We are satisfied and need not struggle.

The whole idea is to simply BE, to align oneself with a world where all is well. Each of us [and the world] would benefit from setting aside a regular inviolate time to simply BE, a time to allow the motor to rest and to simply enjoy the peace of the moment without having to go anywhere or do anything or change anything. To use your current language and something similar, you once heard from R. Zalman, "We cannot run the motor all the time at high speed and expect the motor to remain like new."[41] As I have witnessed, humans in your period of history have so much calling to you all the time that even when you think you are resting, you are not. The best you can do is to idle your motor. If not, turn it off.

Some choose this time according to a religious schedule, but what of those who do not have a religion with time set aside?

---

[41] Rabbi Zalman Schacter Shalomi z"l was a prominent rabbi of the twentieth and twenty-first centuries (b.1924, d.2014). He was part of the Hassidic movement and went on to found Jewish Renewal.

Then, it is important to schedule such a time. The time does not have to be the same every week, but the regularity of a weekly ritual set aside for holy time and space is highly beneficial to the body, mind, and spirit. Time and space set aside are sacrosanct and inviolate. The mind and body can rest from worldly activities, and the spirit, in turn, rests with them. With rest, new pathways in the brain and the spirit have the time and the peaceful rest to develop.

The full observance of the Sabbath in my day and community was a time during which we seriously took the receiving of our second soul, the *Shechinah* [the feminine aspect of God and the manifestation of the Divine presence on Earth], and Divine guidance and inspiration. We did not merely observe the laws of Shabbat but were privy to the inner world of the Sabbath in which one can only reside by intention rather than by action or inaction. [By intention, I mean observance of the laws and *meaning* of the Sabbath.] We were also very aware of the *Neshama Yetirah*[42] that is gifted for the duration of the Sabbath. It was especially during those times that we received our spoken Divine guidance and insights into the lineage of our souls and within the Jewish tradition/history.

It was a common practice during this period to discover the names of those in whom our souls had been present throughout our history. The lineage was spiritual rather than generational. We inherited their positive actions and traits along with what

---

[42] The *Neshama Yetirah* is considered the second soul but is more properly translated as the expanded soul. This is a concept that comes from early Kabbalistic writings. It is said that this second, or expanded soul enters the body with the onset of Shabbat and departs after the Shabbat ends (26 hours).

called for correction. The 26 hours of the Sabbath began by welcoming the Sabbath dressed in white and the field as our beloved *Shechinah* approached with the setting of the sun. This practice was an innovation of our day. We incorporated physical activity with our spiritual practice and religious rituals.[43] These were intended to bring the Divine Light further into our beings so that we could more intensely and completely serve the purpose of bringing the Divine Light into the World. Though the *Shechinah* [known as both the feminine aspect of God and the Bride of Shabbat — *likrat kallah*] would remain only for the duration of Shabbat, her residual Light lasted us until the next Shabbat [for those who chose to hold it]. So, too, did some of the Light remain that came with the Divine guidance that was channeled on Shabbat. This assisted us in our ability and our motivation to continue the work that we did. It was with every breath that the Light was with us, and we often had difficulty in life balancing such an amount of Light with the mundane aspects of our lives. It was the fuel for our engines.

---

[43] HaAri's custom of going to the field and facing the setting sun was augmented by the composition of Shlomo HaLevi Alkabetz (1500-1576) to welcome the Sabbath Bride, *L'ch Dodi*.

TO BE OF THIS WORLD

August 18, 2019

Ah ha! You have discovered quite a treasure trove of information today, and there will be more, of course. There is much more to read in the first text, and then we will go over it. You already know that some of it is not exactly correct, but it has led you to some commentary from me with clues for further discoveries. You have found evidence of my deep interest and involvement in the study of alchemy[44] and that I was a proponent of the scientific method. There are many surprises for those who closely study us [our circle from Safed] and our surprising range of interests. Things remain undiscovered, even to this day. You may want to read what I have written on alchemy, but it is not essential just yet.

You also noticed that my adherence to the scientific method was made known to the world outside my inner circle. For as far as we traveled in our quest for Unification with the One, we were also grounded in this world of materiality. We managed to carry these things with a fine balance. Not only did we have to appear

---

[44] Eliezer Brodt, "R. Chaim Vital and his Unknown Work Sefer ha-Pe'ulot: A Work on Science, Medicine, Alchemy and Practical Magic," July 8, 2010, accessed October 20, 2022, https://www.academia.edu/37197602/R_Chaim_Vital_and_his_Unknown_Work_Sefer_ha_Peulot_pdf.

as though we were of this world, but we had to actually BE of this world. In part, this was to be effective in bringing about the changes with which we were tasked. Also, it was to give credence to others that we were flesh and blood, in a way, like them. That is especially important as you have known for quite a while; we must look, walk, talk, participate, and achieve like those who are what society deems as "everybody else" [or "normal"]. This is usually necessary to be accepted. Well, at least that is what we thought — and it is what you still think. It is not as true in your day. There is much more room in today's world for individuality. Even in the closed communities, there is more room for this than in my day — not everywhere, but increasingly so.

Some things about me have not yet been discovered and may never be. I will tell you much, but — well, we will see.

———◆———

Now, to comment on the work that you are reading about HaAri and me, It says that I contradict ideas and facts within the context of my writings. This is true and also deserves a somewhat reiterated explanation. As I have mentioned before, my writings were taken from me[45] and copied with errors. Compounded upon that, when those copies were read by those who thought they knew HaAri and what he meant to say, they took it upon themselves to further edit the already adulterated copies. Of

---

[45] It is reported in various sources (some differ slightly in the details) that while R Hayyim Vital was quite ill (at about the age of 47), either his brother or his son (varying reports) gave a large selection of his written works to a third party who then distributed them to a large number of copyists. The copies were made in a matter of a few days and the originals were then returned to the home of R. Hayyim.

course, there appeared to be many contradictions. Also, as time progressed and my personal knowledge was expanded, I felt some things needed to be revised and corrected by me because they no longer held true in my judgment.

It was a time of discovery and experimentation and transformation of practice and ideas. In spite of my own abilities, I was most definitely under the extreme influence and in a state of awe of the great master. [It was not something that he directed toward me, but it was an attraction that was vibrational, beyond space and time and human understanding. I want to make this known that it was not even of this world.] I remained in this same state of awe all the years after his passing, but I slowly realized my strength and skills. Paradoxically, I also doubted myself to a debilitating degree. It was an odd experience to feel such awe and deference and yet know that this feeling was also my "home."

Although I knew of R. Isaac Luria to an extent before he actually arrived on the scene in Safed, I did not know just how easy it would be for me and everyone else to get lost in his presence once he was physically among us. The increasingly expanded consciousness that I experienced during the time that I spent with him only grew as the years of my life took me on to yet more expansive experiences of the mind and spirit. To see this world and our existence from higher realms — the places where our souls traveled — and to experience the fact that this world is not all there — that it is indeed a world of illusion — is indescribable, and one is never the same after such an experience. Each additional exposure to such vision and heights of spirit is something that is at once glorious beyond measure and isolating when one returns to the mundane. To live with one foot in each world is a very tricky balancing act indeed.

These extra-worldly experiences tended to isolate me from others with whom I associated. [I believe that some now call this astral projection or inter-dimensional travel — although I would equate astral travel only to the journey and not the ultimate destination.] Of course, there was never another with whom I could share the inner worlds in the same way that I could with HaAri, but I did make attempts. Possibly, I succeeded in teaching others the ways of learning about the process, with all its formulas and textual references, and having the personal experience of *Yichud* and all of the glorious stops along the way. For even if one would not reach that ultimate destination of Unification, the stops along the way were destinations and experiences in and of themselves. I must state that too many people lie, steal, and cheat themselves out of the experiences available to them. To see only reaching the destination as the marker of success and enlightenment is to deny oneself the major joys and lessons of the experience. It always made me sad to see them do this, and I will not say that it was done maliciously (except by a few), but, in doing so, they cheated themselves out of the experiences that were true for them. This is a common occurrence in spiritual journeying, and you see this today as well.

Some want it so much that they degrade and deny their own experience by adopting someone else's. They think that the experience of the other is superior in some way, much as the way people wish for the abilities of another, and, in doing so, are blind to their own gifts. No one is helped in such a case, neither the envied nor the envier. Any genuine experience that they do have is diminished by their participation in this activity. I have to admit that though I did not envy my teachers in life, my extreme awe of them diminished my abilities in my own eyes and denied me much. As these masters receded from my everyday life [because I outlived most of them], I gained momentum in the direction of my life's mission and felt capable and committed to making my imprint on what was passed on to me. Yet I did not fulfill the full complement of my duties in life, and so yes, there were contradictions and discrepancies in the works and also in my life. Now, I have explained this matter in a general way.

In this work we are writing together, I will continue contradicting some things I have previously put to paper. This is the main reason for our endeavor. You read about the theory that there were five different levels of Lurianic thought, and I have already explained to you that this was a way that HaAri reached more of his students [and succeeding generations]. Had he taught all at his highest level, he would have lost most of his audience. Likewise, if he had taught to the lowest common denominator [and I do not like to say it in that way], he would have lost many of his more or most advanced students. Some teachers do not separate the levels as distinctly, but he allowed each group to think that the teachings they received were at the top level and, therefore, most valid —and for them, they were. In each group, there were those [as there always are] who understood in their way and not exactly as the teachings intended. So, there you have it. Surprisingly, the teachings have been reduced to *only* five levels, for each of the students then taught the ideas according to their own understanding.

As you read the increasingly complex explanations of creation and emanations and all the ensuing expounding and weaving of theoretic threads, you may see that the complexities are far too intricate and can only be understood by a very select few or that the complexities are possibly unnecessary to understand the wonder and awe and "magic" of creation and all it involves. There are many who become lost and wander forever in the explanations and the theories and the intricacies of it all and miss the deepest experience of it. At times, I, too, was guilty of that. Sadly, there were times when I forgot the inner tools necessary to make the journey, free of explanations and all the rest of the unnecessary thoughts that transpire in the human mind. This can take away from the ecstasy and inexplicable sensation of knowing the Divine with the entirety of your being.

One can read all the materials and all the words and methodologies of any master, but in the matter of the spirit, it is the willingness and the faith to live the experience that takes one forward in the direction of Unification. Too many need the connection of the human verbal construct to keep themselves tethered to their here and now when it is precisely (and only) the letting go of the here and now that allows for the full experience. All the book learning and all the words are not what helps one "lift off the ground." All the book learning and words do not matter unless one has the willingness to leave them behind and just go for the ride.

August 21, 2019

It is not linear, this project of ours, and it need not be. You are concerned that it will not be of interest or hold people's interest if it is not linear, and yet you are not at all linear. Our work will proceed as it does now, and I will speak as the thoughts occur to me so you are guided in transcribing my words. I speak much of how times change, that innovation is necessary [though human nature does not change so much], and yet you are the one who clings to forms of the past. We shall venture forth in the way we have been going with this.

I want to talk more about the transitions of leadership in my time and into new ideas, and why it was so incredibly easy. The RaMaK was an incredibly kind and patient teacher of all that was traditional in the law, practices, and texts of Judaism. I found his kindness equal to his sagacity and knowledge of the tradition and the texts. He created an atmosphere of dedicated learning and of dedicated, passionate learners, where we all participated in the teaching and the learning at the same time. One could feel his embrace as he kept us [his students] close and comfortable while, at the same time, he excited, inspired, and activated us. No area of study was unwelcome in his circle. (Remember, of course, that I am speaking of the studies of topics mainly within the confines of Jewish study.) With the RaMaK, life was orderly, made sense, and was intellectually exciting and safe. Safe was the life I had known.

Intellectually, I had always lived in an expanding yet safe world. Life was full, full of the expected. The only area that did not feel safe to me was the arena of personal relationships, as I have mentioned before. There was a degree of emotional immaturity and lack of judgment in some of my life that I never overcame, despite all that I achieved in my lifetime. I had a certain degree of naïveté that for the most part, served me well, but many times it created a gap between me and others who did not understand my nature. There were some who tried to take advantage of me [some succeeded] and some who kept their distance from me because of this. For those who loved me, my innocence was an endearing trait. HaAri spoke of it as a most precious gift indeed. Those in the world around me did not know about this unless they were quite close to me. Some thought I was an unusual, kind, and wise man, but there was something different about me. There was. People are generally wary of what is different and of the people they do not see themselves reflected.

I was comfortable in the RaMaK's circle, and it would have been hard not to be, as it was his nature to create that feeling amongst his students. All were welcome who had the heart and mind for true study and devotion to the life created in our community. We were like family (complete with family issues). That there was a personal link between the RaMaK and HaAri, though for no more than a moment in time, was a great help in facilitating the transfer of leadership in this learning community. Not only was the community/group pathway facilitated, but the shift in focus in the way of understanding the teachings of Zohar and Kabbalah was also able to move forward. The RaMaK had created the systematic cataloging of Kabbalistic knowledge,[46] which was the basis for HaAri's, allowing for amplified understandings and experiential knowledge of the material that came before him. The work gave a firm foundation to even those who wished to begin understanding the advanced flights of HaAri.

---

[46] See his book, *PaRDeS Rimonim* (*Garden of the Pomegranates*).

It seemed as though what he taught had indeed been born along with the essence of his being, and I believe that it had always lay within him. Much of it was activated during his time of self-isolation on the island of the Nile and his time there with Elijah.[47] I believe that Elijah continued the awakenings within him throughout his life, and by doing this, he facilitated the flow of information so that it would emanate from him continually, even after his passing. Perhaps this was the reason that the Light so easily flowed from him. It was continuous, that aura of Light, both around him and in his eyes. What you are feeling now in your body and soul at this moment as you write is what was felt in his presence. It was an almost indescribable inner joy that was like a turning up of one's life force. It was joyful, motivational, and life-giving and something that one could easily become addicted to. I did. I was at my fullest, my bravest, my most alive, not only in his presence but for the rest of my life whenever I brought him into my consciousness. I continued to carry his presence with me and convey his ideas through teaching and writing. This essence permeated my work. There were times that his presence withdrew from me after his passing due to my actions or inactions. I refer to this in my book *Sefer HaHezyanot (The Book of Visions)*.

It was when in his presence, and later with the remainder of his energy that was left behind with me [that is not technically true, but I am not sure what words to put to this], which powered many others as well, besides me.

---

[47] He spent approximately six years in relative isolation on an island in Cairo belonging to his uncle, Mordechai Francis. There he spent his days meditating and studying the Zohar, seeing his family only on Shabbat. There, the prophet Elijah came to him as a guide and teacher and remained with him throughout his days on Earth.

In the bare second that it took for HaAri to step into the leadership position and begin to teach us shortly after his arrival, I took a step back for a second. It has been widely reported that I avoided R. Yitzhak Luria upon his arrival in Safed and for a time after that. They had no way of knowing the Truth of the matter, which is something I speak of elsewhere in this volume. My emotions were such that after the passing of the RaMaK, I was reluctant to accept a new teacher, especially so quickly. My emotions and my grief caused me to hold back from accepting this transition of alliances. It was not really a switching of alliances, but that is what I thought at the time. Another piece that held me back was something that often occurs with humans. We, to varying degrees, resist [or are not yet consciously aware of] what we know is best for us, what is inevitable. I knew that Rabbi Isaac Luria was to be in my future, just as he knew that I would be in his. All of this was not at a conscious level. The difference was that he did not resist what he knew to be Truth; I sometimes [often] ran from it. For some, the stronger the draw is, the more deliberately they run in the opposite direction. You and I share this to a degree. It is a fact that is sadly true for many. What some run hardest toward is not good for them, and what some run hardest away from is in their best interest. Yet, this is another aspect of human behavior that does not change.

August 22, 2019

Add to what was written yesterday that the aura surrounding HaAri was such that it was like no other that we had encountered. Not even with the likes of all the luminaries in our midst did we experience energy such as that which emanated from him.

Sometimes I think [later in my life did I think this] that even though he had grown into this power of his, it had increased exponentially upon his arrival in Safed, and at times, that came as a surprise even to him. With all that he had studied, learned, and experienced in his life, I do not believe he expected the ramping up of his abilities and knowledge in the way it occurred upon his arrival. [It was as if he had gotten what you call an upgrade to his power system. Did it just take the proper environment to recognize and appreciate what was already present in him? Do we each have a place, situation, or person who serves as the one or the thing that is that which serves as the main switch to turn on our main transformer? Or is it that our resistance to the wholeness of our being is removed?] He followed what had been told to him by Elijah about moving to Safed and making me his primary student, yet he was not sure what awaited him there other than expecting me as a student. I believe that his powers and knowledge expanded on the journey, and then upon arrival in Safed, it was as if he came into full bloom.

After all (yet unbeknownst to anyone at the time), he would not have much more time on Earth to make the impact that he had come into this world to create. It seems that if he knew everything else under the sun, the moon, and of all the heavens, he must have known this too. This will remain somewhat of a mystery, which, if asked about, he would respond with a quiet, enigmatic smile and a look of kindness directly into your eyes, saying, "Think what you like." He would then close his eyes, draw into himself, and a moment later, he would continue with whatever conversation we had been having. Such was the genuine humility of the man. Keep in mind that we were all still relatively young at this time. [I was 29, and he was 36.] We were not yet old men who had been wizened by life and experience and who, more often than not, knew the right thing to say or do.

Our circle had our study, our work [most of us], our wives, and our children, and we were trying to be what we believed the Almighty had created us to be. And, of course, we were also trying to find ways to bring on the Messianic Age, save the world, and, if not that, at least redeem the Jewish people. So, we were young and had a lot on our shoulders and minds. We felt the pressure of all these things, and yet we also knew that of utmost importance was to create new ways to enter the new era so that others might continue the work. We also knew that we had to experience what we were teaching ourselves before passing it on to others. The last part was mostly experienced by HaAri and me and, on occasion, one or two others. The work that we did was often experimental, and we had to proceed with caution. Well, I had the caution, and he had complete faith.[48] It is imperative to take great caution concerning who participates in such activities, as we wish only good as a result from and for them.

The excitement of being around his energy allowed me to enter his world for periods of time and also to enter a new world for myself, for I had been staid and traditional until the point that I met him. For most of my life, I experienced varying degrees of discomfort that I could not quite explain — just being in the world was like wearing a suit of clothes that did not fit.

In all my studies, from the time I was a child, I had felt a pull to something greater beyond the traditional studies in which I was

---

[48] See "Four Who Entered the Garden" in the Appendix.

so involved. Something pulled me elsewhere, and I was not often quite present in my studies (or my body), even though my mind and voice produced the answers my teachers requested of me. And with my personal life as well, it was like this. I could participate for a time, but I would become uncomfortable when a feeling of there being something else, something greater calling to me, arose within me. With the arrival of this man, Rabbi Isaac Luria, in my life, I felt as though I had arrived at the place that had been pulling at me or drawing me forth my whole life. Perhaps that was the real reason for my reluctance to join him when he arrived in Safed. As I mentioned, so many resist their destiny when it appears before them, even when they have been drawn to it for a lifetime.

This running away, you know about it. It did not last as long for me as it has for you. [Although, for me, it was a recurrent theme throughout and until the end of my life.] Running away from that which we are destined is as familiar to you as it was to me. It is a universally familiar theme. Our texts [for example, Jonah] show us this situation repeatedly since it is a natural response in humans. Some never stop running, or at least they turn away from that which they came into life to accomplish. [This does not mean that they accomplish nothing; it just means that they will need to return][49] to achieve that which only they can, in their uniqueness, contribute to the world.

From my present perspective, I will say that the mission of each individual's lifetime is rarely singular and relegated only to that particular lifetime. There may be many small pieces to their

---

[49] To the same situation in the present lifetime or reincarnate in another lifetime.

puzzle and maybe a few larger ones or their mission may be, in fact, singular and brief. Now, I will say that there is no action that does not ripple out in some way, so the piece or pieces of the mission need not be large to have maximum effect. One can complete life feeling that their mission was not accomplished or, in fact, that there was no mission to be accomplished. The majority of people do not even consider the fact that they have a mission — a destiny, yes, but not a mission. While some may just go about doing what they do, they may consider their destiny to be doing one thing or another or being in one condition or another. They may never consider that they were in the exact right place at the exact right time to fulfill their purpose on Earth. They may be annoyed by their circumstance or merely accept it as God's will and never consider anything beyond that. They will nevertheless be accomplishing their mission. Most missions are not of an earth-moving magnitude, at least not to the holder of the mission. Again, because of the nature of your technology and worldwide broadcasting of everything, people are more aware of their purpose and want theirs to be the biggest, the most fulfilling, and the most powerful. This leads to what I spoke of earlier concerning inauthentic reporting of their journeys and, in that way, leading others to the same path of inauthenticity.

August 23, 2019

I am with you much more of the time than just when we are writing, but you know this. It is not only the writing that motivates my relationship with you. I experience the world when I connect with you. You notice that I enjoy it when you write in public, and this is because I have a chance to share in more than just your solitary experience.

You will be able to continue this work when you return home because I will make sure of it. And you will see new places. We will see new places together. We will see many places together, both here and there, and other places you have not yet imagined being on your itinerary. You know you will have to take credit for this book, which will be one of the biggest steps you have ever taken in your life, so get ready.

Yes, you will soon be in the most extreme expansion of your life. All will be well if you do not resist it. This is a platform you will walk on, and you will keep walking even when there is no platform under your feet that you can see. You will continue to be supported, and in your mind and heart, you know this to be true. It is time. You can feel yourself gaining strength, and soon enough, it will translate to the physical. You will gain strength as you gain enthusiasm and courage by stepping out of yourself and extending your hand of Light out into the world. Some of this you will do on your own in the world outside your room, and some you will be able to do in a private setting with the help of my instruction.

HaAri will come to you again and will have some information for you. The meditative adventures we will embark on will bring you to new and expanded parameters in the universe, both inside and outside your being. You are already preparing for this adventure as you seem to be resting a lot. You are doing much more than you think. You are preparing yourself. Things will change, and all for the good. You are bringing new understandings into your consciousness necessary for the changes ahead. Just keep up with what you are doing, and yes, you will be getting out a bit more.

August 25, 2019

Many authentic spiritual [and other] teachers deconstruct what they instinctively know so that others might benefit from the natural knowledge within a teacher's being. [This knowledge is not necessarily taught or studied in a class.] To do this, not only must the teacher possess the knowledge but also the gift of creating and articulating a simplified and comprehensible deconstruction [that is, an instruction manual]. Not all teachers have the skills to communicate the information to which they have been privy within the confines of their minds. Some teachers require the assistance of one who understands their ideas and work and who possesses the skills to spell out the information to a larger audience. HaAri was one of these men, and I was the one he needed.

When teaching a small group or one-on-one, no one was more brilliant than he. He could reach into [yes, inside] his students to deliver the message to them in a way that they alone were able to hear and understand. And this happened with each student, even when they were in a group. But when writing the information, he became too intricate and enmeshed in his explanations, and the information began to weave itself into more complicated patterns the more he wrote. It was as though that which came forth from him was like the silk thread produced by a spider with which he spins his web, and the patterns would become more and more intricate, though they need not have been so. The thread of explanation kept coming forth endlessly, and the web became exquisitely beautiful, but the prey could have been caught efficiently with much less effort. There was no end to the source of the material for the thread that HaAri could produce.

Sadly, it is not so helpful to most people to receive such a complex creation. I was the vehicle for explaining his works and breaking them down in a much simpler way than he could accomplish. This may seem difficult to believe since much of my writing seems quite complex, but it was — and is — true. Having read some of my works, can you imagine I was considered to be the one who wrote simply? You, yourself, sometimes weave too dense a web when you write, but that will not work for our purposes, so we will work together on this effort to simplify.

August 26, 2019

A most difficult lesson for me was (and still is, it seems) that I must learn to give bites, provide time and space to chew on them, and not offer another bite until they have been swallowed. I also see that this is perhaps even more difficult than knowing what information to begin with. You have listened to many teachers in your time. When they impart their knowledge to those who come to learn, some will comprehend and learn the lessons, some will take away perhaps one or two things, and yet others will wonder if they fell asleep during the teaching because they heard none of it. [In some cases, they do fall asleep.] Hopefully, all who read this will find something that touches their mind or spirit, and hopefully both.

This work is more of a conversation between you, me, and the reader. Hopefully, we will answer questions that readers did not necessarily even know they had. And that is a good thing.

August 27, 2019

The material from the greatest teachers flows from the teacher's soul to the student's soul. This is one reason it is difficult to transmit these teachings in writing. The soul of true teachers knows what to teach at the right moment that it needs to be taught. They receive the words to use, but also a transmission, a transferring vibration to embed the lesson within the student. Such teachers know when the soul of the student is open to receiving. You see, the mind may not remember or fully comprehend the lesson, but the soul takes away from it all that is necessary.

There were many occasions on which HaAri delivered his lessons without any words at all, and those, too, I could translate into words. You see, and I know you do see, that the transmissions that come via thought are sometimes the most powerful and the most necessary [as the constraint of words does not limit them]. Many things are taught to us by angels or guides as we sleep. These are some of the deepest messages and lessons of all. Although we may not remember them with our conscious mind, they lay dormant beneath the surface until such time as we have a need for them]. But, if they are to be proliferated and passed on, most likely, they will need words put to them. And that is where people like me, Hayyim Vital, and you [and many others] come in.

In my time, many of us had teachers who came to us in thought form [for lack of a better term at the moment]. What can I say but that these teachers were energy, spirit, vibrational, multi-dimensional, prophetic, angelic, personal, and more? They came to us regularly as individuals and also spoke through us to the others in our circle. The information they gave us individually was always through these thought patterns, and many of us could transcribe their messages in diaries. These diaries were usually private, with the greatest exception being the Maggid Meisharim[50] of Yosef Karo z"l. This was the most famous and the most documented of our messengers. As for me, I documented some of my transmissions in my diary and spiritual autobiography, *Sefer HaHezyanot*.

I know now that many throughout history have received information, advice, and instruction from a variety of energies. Each cultural group describes and explains the phenomenon in the way that makes the most sense to them, although this is not generally accepted in most modern Western cultures. Nevertheless, it does exist all over the world, and I will tell you that it is happening more and more in your time. It is a way in which people, more and more people, are learning information these days that is necessary for the future of humankind. And if they do not receive the information themselves, they can glean the information from others who do receive and speak of or publish it. Due to the abundance of such activity, discernment is of utmost importance to screen out interference from ego and inauthentic sources. This is one of the reasons I have come to have you speak for me rather than on my behalf: to teach perhaps a bit about another time and place and culture [for some] firsthand and to point out that the things we think are written in stone in our time may shift as times change. Even that which we preach as the definitive paths to Truth, we later find not to be so definitive.

---

[50] See "The Maggid of Joseph Karo" in the Appendix.

Ultimate Truth *does not change* — *ever!* From a higher and non-human perspective, the pathways are almost infinite, but they all lead to the same Truth. Without the input coming from non-corporeal sources [that is, energies not currently contained within a living body on the Earth], it is difficult for humans to break out of their stringent ways of thinking. Even many forward thinkers are greatly constrained in their abilities to expand to the extent necessary for forward movement at a rate that will be helpful to humankind. We are giving you a push.

August 28, 2019

I spoke to you of the voices — the teachers who came to us to guide us, inform us, and lead us in the direction that would be best for us to follow. When we heeded them, all went well. We were never led astray. Life and our mission advanced smoothly with their assistance. Some of the teachers advised on the methods and technologies being devised to achieve our previously mentioned goals, some helped to increase our understanding of the sacred texts [Zohar, *Sefer HaBahir*, *Sefer Yetzirah*, and others], and some advised on the personal life and the struggles we encountered while traveling our respective and collective paths. And then there was Yosef Karo's Maggid, who advised him even on the most minuscule of daily tasks.[51]

---

[51] "It is I who speaks with you, your soul {neshama}, not the nefesh nor the ruach, but rather the neshama herself. And is it not so, if prophesy has ceased from Israel, from you it has not ceased, for each time I come to you to direct you in which way to go."

It is one thing to listen to the voice as it speaks in a moment separate and apart from daily and routine activities, and it is quite another to learn to listen on a more regular and ongoing basis to achieve maximum benefit and integration of what the guidance offers. There is a practice of recording in writing the messages one hears, but that may not lead to personal integration of the material or listening deeply on an ongoing basis. You know this to be true in your own life, as you often do not consciously remember the information given to you as you go through the day. Those who communicate with us authentically and in our best interest provide us with experiences and reminders throughout the day to bring to our awareness what they have previously told us. It takes training and conscious attention to sense the presence of this kind of advice, assistance, and opportunity.

This is no longer the purview of exclusively gifted spiritual leaders and the few gifted with what you call psychic abilities. In fact, your world is discovering an unlimited number of people with psychic abilities. It is interesting that the number of people resistant to the idea is somewhat in correspondence with the number of people admitting to possessing these abilities. There are still many holdouts, but as the numbers grow, you will witness a variety of changes in your world. You are already seeing much upheaval. I was ready to tell you of this almost fifteen years ago when I first contacted you, and what was then the future was not

---

See the Maggid. *The statement of the Maggid* (Venice, 47a, Zalkwa, 51b), "Authenticity of Maggid Mesharim," *Stack Exchange*, accessed August 27, 2022, https://judaism.stackexchange.com/questions/56940/authenticity-of-maggid-mesharim.

so evident. Now, most people can see the upheaval clearly as the changes are speeding up and are in evidence.

In my time, each culture engaged its elite in these types of "foretelling" messages, but as I say, they were few and far between and revered rather than reviled. Now that there are so many more engaged by the messages that flow forth into your world, there is more danger of something I spoke of a few days ago. There are those who engage in disingenuous transmissions. Either they are creating the messages out of their desire, or they may be subject to messages that come from sources other than pure intention. Either way, in this world of yours, which makes airtime and exposure available to all, this can be dangerous.

There are many who do not believe that they, too, are meritorious to receive this coaching from what they call the great beyond, and so they depend on others to fill their cup. They are thirsty, and so they drink what is served to them. Yes, you remember Shabbatai Tzvi was the same. People were thirsty for leadership and passage to a greater future, but he was but one man [two really], and now the world is bigger, more densely inhabited, and much thirstier. How much more so today that people will fall into the trap of the fictitious spiritual message? Some messages are not exactly false but simply repackaged versions of previously gleaned Wisdom. As long as the messages are of genuine Wisdom and Truth and not fakery, they affect only the distributor and not the ones who receive the Wisdom. If the one receiving the information is not coming from a place of Love and Light and for humankind's true benefit, he damages himself and many others. This is also the case of one who manufactures information to suit his own purposes. The one that makes up the information to suit his purposes is, of course, guilty to an even greater degree than one who is simply not based on Love and the Light.

The world is vulnerable now. This means it is very thirsty and must be careful about the well from which it drinks.

August 29, 2019

We will continue in the way of yesterday's transmission. So, I repeat the question of how one distinguishes between a genuine and an inauthentic message. It is quite simple, really. Only authentic messages resonate with Love and are for your well-being and best interests. If there is any detection of negativity within the message of the voice, it is not of a Divine nature. If you receive direction to speak hurtful words or act in any way that would be harmful to you and others, then it is not of a Divine nature and is not to be heeded. You may not like a message because you are not in alignment with Love at the moment, but you will be able, in any event, to recognize if it is for your best and highest good or not. If the message does not come from a place of Love, *do not listen*! Simple.

REINCARNATION

September 1, 2019

There are some things I would like to address at this point that are more specific than what I have discussed up until now. Some of these things have been on hold while you waited for helpful research materials on these topics. Aha! Now you see the time has come since you easily found and already possessed the book you needed! And you had been searching for so long. When the time is right, we know it because all we need is laid before us.

As you perceive from an initial and superficial look at the material in the book, *Sefer Shaar HaGilgulim [The Book of the Gate of Reincarnation]*, what strikes you is the extreme amount of meticulous detail contained in its pages. As we look at specific areas, you will discover what I have to say about each thing, and we may simplify some of what is written. First, though, we must discuss authorship attribution. I said before the line sometimes disappeared between HaAri's work and my own. There was not a subject known to me that the two of us did not discuss, and we discussed this theme in extreme detail and at great length on a great number of occasions [as well as having engaged in experiential research. Perhaps I will provide details later.].

The ramifications of the details under the subject of reincarnation are pertinent to our past, present, and future history. Reincarnation concerns the very fabric of humankind and the world. The book as written is my work, but I will say that much of it came from deep considerations and conversations during my time with HaAri and others. It is my work, as I wrote it, and it flowed forth from me, but it is impossible to separate the waters from two rivers once they have flowed together. So, was it my work? Yes, it was without a doubt, and it included the input of colleagues and my teachers. There should no longer be any issue about authorship in the religious and academic worlds. In the end, the information and its Truth are what are important, but there is [and was] too much focus put on the lesser of important aspects, such as the disputation of authorship.

I was given both less credit and more credit in the world as a result of my association with HaAri. Mostly, it was not an issue to me during my lifetime, but it is something I see, as you would say, "in the rear-view mirror." This is something that happens time and again throughout history and will continue. I am bringing it up here so that you and the readers know it as part of my story.

Let us focus first on the generalities of reincarnation as presented in *Sefer Shaar HaGilgulim*. Let me say that those who were at times satisfied [for a few seconds at least] to simply exist in the world with no explanation of absolutely anything, to experience the world and the cosmos through nothing more than breathing in and out the *Ruach Elohim* [Breath of God] within us — we espoused too much complexity of the workings of just about everything. It was not intended to be exclusionary but rather a way of explaining what had been exquisitely explained to us by our teachers from other worlds. Allow me to say that for us, the explanations did not seem so complex, but anyone who did not hear them directly from Source found them so. Even those familiar with the vocabulary and the basic concepts could not completely grasp the material, as the nuances of the explanation were impressed upon our minds, and souls remained inaccessible to those who did not receive it directly from Source. It is this way with so many ideas that are divinely inspired and brought into this world via the mind of a human being who is overly immersed in the topic at hand. [And if he was not totally immersed before the revelation, he is after it.] The person who will be interested, familiar with, and otherwise qualified to translate the thoughts into words and transmit them to others [but not always].

I mentioned in an earlier transmission about the translation of ideas into verbal language. So much is lost in the deconstruction of these thoughts into words. Humans may or may not have the talent to transmit information. But some material exceeds the gifts of even those who are gifted. The abundance and complexity of the topic of Revelation can overwhelm human capabilities. At the time this material was written, we thought [collectively] that these verbose and complex explanations were necessary for various reasons — among them so that only the most learned would have access to the information, and even they might be discouraged given its complexity.

September 2, 2019

It may be that all of what was written on the transmigration of the soul was, and is, true and complete, but the majority is not necessary to explain or know in the human world.

The general nature of the trajectory, the mission of the soul, and all its emanations and fractalated partitioning and stops along the way into its three-dimensional existence have been endlessly discussed. There are stops along the way as the soul descends from [the realm of] the Source of All Creation into the physical world and all the levels within the levels. [The same is true for its ascent.] The process is documented in an extraordinary amount of detail, in words and visions that were received by us.

As I speak of this to you, it occurs to me an extraordinary complexity, no matter how much one tries to simplify. What does one leave out? How does one synthesize such enormity and complexity of detail? The story of each soul is traced according to 1) from where it originates, 2) what it needs to accomplish on Earth to achieve rectification, and 3) the path on which it needs to travel back to the place from which it emanated and, if and when it will return to a body [in what form, for how long, and for what purpose].

September 3, 2019

To reexplain and simplify all this is like deconstructing a most complex and elaborately woven fabric to decide which of the threads to use in weaving a new fabric — one that will also be beautiful and serve more or less the same purpose as the more elaborate one. Both materials will cover you and keep you warm and protected, and they use the same basis, the threads, so their essential nature is the same. Still, one can be worn on a more regular basis and one only in the highest courts. Both serve their purpose, although the person who would wear one would not necessarily wear the other.

Despite the differences in the levels of articulation of the whole process, the process itself is not changed, just the understanding of it. The explanation of *gilgul* [reincarnation] that appears in the pages of *Shaar HaGilgulim* is like the exquisite robe worn in the highest court. The vision we received, which was beyond words, is what was worn in the Holy of Holies in the Celestial Temple.

In your time, when you see a rocket blast off into space, you can appreciate the beauty and wonder of the event and know the rocket has lifted off and headed to space. Even if you do not understand what the operators are trained to do, the mechanical and electrical details of the rocket's launch and operation, or the experiments done during the trip, you can still appreciate the beauty of the launch, the fact that there are humans in space and that you will most likely reap the eventual benefits of the scientific experiments they perform on their journey. And so this is analogous to our transmigration of the soul and reincarnation, which will continue without the reader being privy to all the details of the process.

The explanation we gave is similar to that offered by other cultures and religions, at least to a degree. Each culture and tradition tribalizes its explanations so its members can better relate to and understand. The actual process was not the point of contention but rather how we articulated the process. We tended to be overly involved in the complexities of not only this but many other processes. Where the dirt road or the trail in the woods may have sufficed to arrive at the destination, we paved a four-lane highway and then gave detailed instructions on the materials and processes that went into the making of it, not to mention the signs along the road.

What I believe will be more interesting to the reader is how this *gilgul* business was readily accepted and even embraced in our circle.

September 8, 2019

Yes, you are seeing evidence today of the nature of the soul and being in contact with your soul and others.[52] This is the evidence in which you revel as you see proof that everything is in order in your present reality. There is comfort in the surprises if one flows downstream with them. "Sure. Hop in the boat," you say. "There's room for everyone." But there is no room in the boat when you sail it upstream against the current; then the boat is all yours.

There is all the evidence you need when you remove the dark glasses and let the Light in so that you can see what is before and all around you. Your world, you can see, is full of evidence of your past, present, and future circumstances. That with which you involve yourself is not always on the road you imagined, but it is your road, nevertheless. Take in the sights and commune with that which draws you in with a high and positive vibration. Take care not to miss the opportunities that inhabit the road to your

---

[52] From the Transcriber: This occurred on a day that I had delivered messages (from "spirit") to people in the café where I transcribed most of the material for this book. It happened on many occasions in the café, that I would be given information to pass along to a patron there. It was a most uncomfortable situation for me but rewarding in the end as the messages always brought not only joy, but most often welcome information that the person had been waiting to hear. This is the soul connection to which R. Hayyim refers.

future. This is when you understand the lessons we teach you — no, of which we remind you — *for you already hold within you all the knowledge that you will need.* You begin to pass these lessons on to others with authenticity and conviction while understanding that this can continue until you sense a resistance that tells you to stop. Whatever penetrates is fine, and whatever does not is fine. You are fine as you are at each moment.

September 9–10, 2019

[53] ויהי נעם אדני אלהינו עלינו ומעשה ידינו כוננה עלינו ומעשה ידינו כוננהו

You read about exorcisms detailed in *Sefer HaGilgulim (The Book of Reincarnation) and Sefer HaHezyanot (The Book of Visions).* What strikes you is the stringency of the questioning addressed to the invading spirit in the process of releasing it and, to a degree, the measures taken against him. Again, the stringency was in keeping with the times and what we knew. It was difficult to deal with these matters within the confines of strictly regulated conventional Judaism. And yet, we dealt with this in keeping with our textual and cultural ways. We resorted to ancient practices and went outside the general [and strict] guidelines of the common practice of our contemporaries in other places in Europe and more halachic[54] mainstream Judaism. In these matters, it is difficult to determine from when exactly some of these basic

---

[53] "And let the beauty of the Lord our God be upon us; and establish the work of our hands upon us; O prosper it, the work of our hands."
Psalm 90:17 from *JPS Hebrew-English TANAKH,* Philadelphia: The Jewish Publication Society, January 1, 2001.
[54] Referring to adherence to Jewish religious law.

practices are derived. They can be found in cultures around the world in some variants of our methods.

Each culture makes the basic practices work within the parameters of what they hold sacred. And, to be honest, our procedure varied depending upon the individual case, circumstances, and those who conducted the "ceremony." The use of amulets and the like was not restricted but mainly used by those of Sephardic background,[55] and it was not unusual for these items to be used for a variety of purposes. [My own father of blessed memory was a master scribe and creator of amulets.] What was used to remove a soul that had invaded the body of a living human included segulot,[56] amulets, smoke, sulfur, candles, the Torah scroll, shofar, psalms 20 & 90, the Ana B'Koach[57] prayer, and other tools and texts — varying somewhat with the individual practitioner. There were specified amulets of protection for the subject of the possession to be worn after the event. It was all within a natural framework for us.

---

[55] Referring to Jews of mainly Spanish or Portuguese descent. They retain their distinctive customs and rituals, preserving Babylonian Jewish traditions rather than the Palestinian ones of the Ashkenazim who are mainly of Eastern European descent.

[56] Segulah (pl.segulot) in this case the word means a remedy or a protection, a benevolent charm – usually written out on paper for the purpose mentioned in the text.

[57] "Ana b'Koach is said to contain the 42-letter name of God, concealed in the first letter of each word in the prayer. The 42 words of Ana b'Koach are split into seven verses of six words each, and the first letter of each of the six words of each line are combined to form one six-letter Divine name, each of which forms aspects or attributes of the 42-letter name ... Ana b'Koach is regarded in the mystical tradition as no less than a portal to the power of creation itself, and to creation's source."
See David Gottlieb, "Ana b'Koach: A Portal to Creation," *My Jewish Learning*, accessed January 20, 2023. https://www.myjewishlearning.com/article/ana-bkoach-a-portal-to-creation/.

There were different methods used to help the invader move on to the next stage of existence as opposed to the different categories of banishing *dybbuks*,[58] who took over the body of a living human for their nefarious purposes — some souls did come into a living body surreptitiously for the purpose of making a *Tikkun* or completing an uncompleted mitzvah. Then, they would graciously exit when done with what they came for without disrupting or damaging the life or body of the human they had used on their holy mission.[59] The *dybbuk*s, on the other hand, were very destructive and caused a great deal of trouble and distress in the human form they occupied, sometimes resulting in the death of the human, as I documented in *Sefer HaGilgulim*. They are angry, unhappy, sinful, destructive, and lost souls participating in this activity. They, too, come to complete something that they left unfinished in this world, but whatever it may be, it is never beneficial for it to be finished. The whole business was very curious and unsettling to me and a matter of immense gravity as well.

---

[58] "[D]ybbuk, a disembodied spirit possessing a living body that belongs to another soul. There are various origins attributed to these spirits. The earliest description usually hinted that they may be nonhuman demons. Later it was assumed they were the spirits of persons who have died. The *dybbuk* may be the soul of a sinner, who wishes to escape the just punishment meted to it by the angels of the grave ... who seek to beat them, or to avoid another form of soul punishment, which is wandering the earth. A *dybbuk* may seek revenge for some evil that was done to it while it lived. Alternatively, it may be lost, and will enter a body simply to seek a rabbi who would be able to help it and send it on its way. The living person may or may not know that a *dybbuk* is occupying his or her body, or it may be tormented by it. This depends on the intent of the possessing soul."
See Llil Arbel, "dybbuk," *Encyclopedia Mythica*, accessed January 20, 2023, https://pantheon.org/articles/d/dybbuk.html.
[59] Now commonly known as a "walk-in."

It is also interesting to me that this type of possession is reported in almost all cultures and throughout time. The gradations represent a full range of experiences from the most minimal [the receiving of thought impressions to channeling helpful and guiding energies] all the way to the very harmful and disabling physical possession by a *dybbuk*. The receiving of helpful messages comes when there is a need and an opening of the consciousness; the channeling comes through openness and merit, and the *dybbuk* just awaits an opening [generally of an innocent] in someone unprotected.[60] There is much to be said about this possession business, but not here and not now.

In the world today, there is a great breakdown of the human spirit, while at the same time, there is also a great awakening. In this paradoxical environment, there is much opportunity to occupy the humans who have allowed their consciousness to fall into an almost full-time nap. There have always been spirits who refuse to travel to their next destination after leaving their body. Some spirits are interrupted in the transition out of the body to continue to their next stop by any one of a number of things, and they need assistance to pass through that consciousness threshold (in which case we who encounter them would speak to them

---

[60] "Most frequently, the unfortunate person whom the dybbuk possessed was a woman. The image of a dybbuk, usually male, penetrating her body is both sexual and an illustration of the doctrine of opposites. Male and female, living and dead, pure and impure, all fused together in one human body. Exorcising a dybbuk, removing the destructive forces from a pure soul, is not just an imperative to save a person who has been possessed. It is a battle in a cosmic war."

See Harry Freedman, "How to deal with a dybbuk," *The JC*, accessed August 28, 2022, https://www.thejc.com/judaism/features/how-to-deal-with-a-dybbuk-1.479193

gently and lead them to the Light that will carry them forward). Most cultures deal with this in much the same manner. Some cultures build this bridging from one realm into the next through their death and funeral practices. But this *dybbuk*, this entity, can itself be possessed, tricked into remaining in its state of inharmonious behavior during his lifetime by forces that wish to wreak havoc in the world.

Souls far from passing into the Light know it and are grateful for the chance not to go. Even though their lives are miserable in many ways and their deeds untold, they do not want to face the unknown possibilities that they feel awaiting them. Their resistance is caused by unfounded fear.[61] Forces of chaos and misaligned energy easily convince these souls to do their bidding, which they make sound much better than what a departing soul expects to face. The Truth is that this would not be what they would face after death, but they do not know that, and they make their choice out of fear — just as they lived their lives in fear. These lost souls are emboldened by the promises made to them in the enticement. As a result, they enter the human subject with great force and determination to do their bidding.

October 1, 2019

And so today, you have begun to read my spiritual autobiography [*The Book of Visions*]. And even in the first few pages, you see much of what I said to you previously. How could I possibly mature and advance normally when I was told so often of the

---

[61] A preponderance of ill-fated experiences is invited by the presence of fear in a person.

elevated state of my soul, my position, and my potential future? It was too much for a child, and, combined with the overwhelming amount of learning thrust upon me, it was no wonder that I had difficulty dealing with interpersonal relationships in society. And it was no wonder that others in my circle, even those who knew me by reputation only, had ideas about me. I say this only to explain who I was as Hayyim, the man. I did the best I could, and I was as kind as I knew how to be.

It was never easy for me to relate to others, perhaps because of who I believed myself to be from what I had been told by so many *hahamim* [sages] and soothsayers, and also from who I felt lived deep inside me. They were two very different people, and I was not able to reconcile the conflict between the two until I met R. Isaac Luria. He and I were as twin souls, and I felt that with him, I was home. Perhaps this is the real reason I resisted him at first. As I have said before, humans often resist that to which they are most attracted. There is a fear of losing oneself, so intense is the draw to the other person. Yes, this was the case for me. Once we found each other, we were better humans for the connection. And when he left me, I lost a part of myself and indeed became confused as to my place in the world without him. Yet, at the same time, I felt I might keep him alive in the world, in my day, and throughout time through my work and even my being.

Sadly, the interpersonal skills I learned from him seemed to all but disappear not long after his passing. And though he would chide me lovingly from time to time from *Olam Habah* [the world to come — the Other Side] to recover those skills, indeed, I was not able to do so for more than a short period. Sometimes I behaved even worse than I did before I had met him. It was a constant struggle for me, and I sometimes became lost in a sea of confusion and struggled just to stay afloat in the world. You see, without HaAri, I had lost my anchor [compass] and my bearings in the world; I had lost the place I called home. What I had learned with him, what he sparked in me, was all that kept me in this world for the remainder of my life.

From the Transcriber
In Hayyim's telling all of this to me, I can feel some of the anguish he carried throughout his life. It was a burden that only his beloved twin soul, Yitzhak, could understand.

HaAri awakened so much that I never realized existed within me. Most importantly, he taught me that all I needed was indeed already within me and only needed to be awakened. But I saw him as the flame that added to the fire of what was just waiting to be reignited, and without that flame, I would have remained but quiet embers. This is true of all humans, but some hold this closer to the surface than others, and it is exactly that which he had hoped to achieve with his work: to increase the flames of as many human candles as he could and to draw out that Light from within each human into the world to bring on the Redemption. That was the simple, profound, and truthful purpose of our work. We were to reclaim the Light that was hidden by the *klippot*. My inner flame burned bright, but I had difficulty bringing it out into the daily light of day.

So, I committed to recording his work and hoped others might be able to achieve this illumination with more success than I did. Conveying his words and thoughts and adding to them was a way for me to achieve my purpose and, to be honest, to keep my personal interactions and difficulties with others to a minimum. It seemed to me the most effective way to keep my soul on a higher level, and it was a more comfortable place for me to be. In my own eyes, it was so hard to live up to all I had been told about myself in my younger years — imagine that all these esteemed and venerated people had told you such things. It is not easy to know where to go with this information or how to act without it affecting you!

October 24, 2019

Regarding *gilgul*[62] and *ibbur*[63]: my ideas on this have evolved and, of course, as with so much else, have expanded to be more universally inclusive and not at all tribal.

---

[62] *Gilgul* – The entry of a soul that has previously incarnated into a newly born being and is permanent (for that lifetime).

[63] *Ibbur* – "The literal translation of the word from Hebrew means 'impregnation.' *Ibbur* is the most positive form of possession, and the most complicated. It happens when a righteous soul decides to occupy a living person's body for a time, and joins, or spiritually 'impregnates' the existing soul. *Ibbur* is always temporary, and the living person may or may not know that it has taken place. Often the living person has graciously given consent for the *ibbur*. The reason for *ibbur* is always benevolent — the departed soul wishes to complete an important task, to fulfill a promise, or to perform a *Mitzva* (a religious duty) that can only be accomplished in the flesh."
See Arbel, "dybbuk." In summary: The entry of a soul into an already living adult body for the purpose of completing some task. (This is almost always a temporary situation that terminates upon completion of the task.)

In my previous work, I limited the possibilities for who might reincarnate into whom and limitations in other categories as well. For instance, there was limiting talk of the transmigration of souls of particular lineages of Torah luminaries who merited the gift of transmigration. Also proposed was that a potential recipient of a soul which entered through the process of *ibbur* had to be of a spiritual level for the soul to enter. *Neither of those things is true.* At the time, I was dealing with my small worldview and now see that even those who lead humble and seemingly unremarkable lives may be at great spiritual levels of development, and lineage does not bear on the process. All are based on the needs and desires of the individual soul at any given time in their development.

MORE ABOUT REDEMPTION

November 3, 2019

You see that you must do no more than focus in the slightest, as in sitting down to read on the topics of my period in history or Kabbalah itself, and you hear me speak to you. The reading, even a few words, shows me that you are ready to receive, and as you know, I am always ready to speak.

You read just enough to spark inspiration and an answer to something you have pondered, though you already knew the answer. The archaic [to you] scenarios of the spiritual journeys of the early Kabbalists, with their images of palaces, waterscapes, and the like, were images of what the people of their time could relate to. Is that what they saw on their journeys to the other worlds? They saw what they could relate to, and with these images, they were able to understand and pass on the information in at least a somewhat understandable frame of reference for their times. Just as it was with the requirement of animal sacrifices was made in the Temple rituals in ancient times — so that the people could relate to new concepts, ideas, and practices within a framework of what was already familiar and common to the surrounding culture — the sages spoke of what was relatable in their time.

And so it was for us, for all who came before us, and all who come after us. There are not always those who can teach what they receive from every generation. Each generation must present the material and the teachings in a way[s] that the people of their time can understand. When the teachings remain in the words and images of old ways and understandings, much may be revered but not understood or followed. That is how many of our teachings come to be lost and, worse still, misunderstood.

When reverence for what once was outweighs an openness to the new, it impedes the way of expansion. Reverence is a good thing to maintain, but too many stop at that point [as if it were the be-all and end-all] and think that the old ways are the only ways.[64] In our time, we revered the laws and customs and abided by them. Look at the works of our beloved and revered Josef Karo and Moses Cordovero. They were masters of the past and codified it all. Yet they were also receptive to what might be transmitted to the openings in our psyches, hearts, and spirits for new ways of understanding the relationship between Almighty God and the created Universe. They listened with reverence to the voices sent to them. And those who listened and heeded provided what you call the tipping point, the pivot into the future.

There is great importance to being knowledgeable and in tune with the history and culture of a time and not just studying the teachings that come out of those years. This importance applies to even the deepest teachings of Universal Truths and Wisdom).

---

[64] Rabbi Avraham Kook (first chief rabbi of Israel/Palestine, circa 1921) said, "Hayashan yithadesh v'hehadash yitkadesh — the old shall be made new, and the new shall be made holy."
See Laurie Fischer, "Parashat Behar, accessed November 7, 2022, https://www.sefaria.org/sheets/234634?lang=bi

It is not that the Truth and Wisdom taught are new but that they are defined by the context of what brought them to the fore and the existing culture. Can their teaching be understood without this historical and cultural context? Probably, but not as well. You have noted that in my speaking to you, I often use expressions and words that relate to your time so that you and those who read this will be able to relate to me and what I have to say in the most thorough way possible.

On many occasions during these writings, I have spoken of the urgent need for redemption in our time. It was that desperate need that drove us so strongly in the direction of finding pathways to redemption. The destruction of some of our most established communities, the annihilation of so many of our people, and the forced emigration and separation of entire populations were so traumatic to the Jewish people that we were fighting for our very survival — both physical and spiritual. It was a time of communal anguish and of the desire for anguish and desperation to end. It was a time of a great desire for liberation and freedom from the various oppressive forces and circumstances to which the world usually subjected us. And we were moved to find a spiritual solution to the general fear and hopelessness of the times. In our minds, it was we who could [and hopefully would] save the Jewish people and the soul of the world.

THE SOUL ROOT AND THE OVERSOUL

December 7, 2019

From the Transcriber

Recorded yesterday, this was an explanation of Soul Root vs. Oversoul. I was reading about Soul Root in the introduction to Book of Visions when I slipped into a distant place, and the voice came through me and recorded. The following is a transcript of that voice recording. I am unsure if the speaker was R. Hayyim.

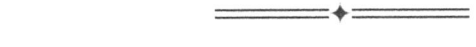

Yes, but you thought wrongly. The Soul Root is different from the Oversoul. The Soul Root is the part of the soul that travels through the time and space dimensions through spiritual, not genealogical, generations. That is the Soul Root. Who were you? Who were you? Who were you? Back and back and back and back. The Soul Root goes through all these time and space beings [incarnations] sequentially.

The Oversoul encompasses so much more in the realm of Nefesh (the basic life force or natural soul in general), and specifically relates to the soul's basic or external manifestations in terms of the faculties of thought, speech, and action. The Oversoul nourishes. It is a nourishment port where the aspects of that soul travel out and out and out and out until the [traveling] capsule has emptied itself of those who wish to enter into a physical being. On the return trip from the world of physical manifestation, other souls are returned to or brought back up to the level of purity. Those souls have no further use for the physical body. I speak of those who have finished that part of their journey or those who will be resting before going back to finish the tasks assigned in the physical world. [The simplicity of this is belied by applying words to the process. There is no simple way to explain the nature of this.] These fragments of the Oversoul travel out [away from the Oversoul] to those into whom they materialize [implant themselves] and maintain the core characteristics and aspects of the soul fragment [of the Soul Root]. They fly out, release their charge, and carry back those who have completed or left their bodies to return to the place where those souls recharge, ripen, and are "harvested."

The Oversoul is where the fragments, or roots, come together. It is their Source, their home. [Would you call this a mothership?] The current/energy that emanates from each of them contributes to making the One. They are all necessary to make the One. That is the activity of the Oversoul, while the Soul Root goes both forward and back in time and space throughout lifetimes. In my case, my lineage was the great sages. Who was I? Whose words did I speak? What value did I have? What value did I give? This is the Soul Root that goes back and back and back in time, through one lifetime and another and another and another. We continued on and on. The Oversoul and the Soul Root are much to digest. I will release you now.[65]

———✦———

The Soul Root permeates time and space and holds the essence of character traits and personality. It determines how we carry out our role or mission in human existence and, in fact, in our soul, our energetic existence. This topic of Soul Root occupied a great deal of our lives, thoughts, and energy! It was very important to us and assisted us in establishing legitimacy in our world. Mostly, ego made us first investigate and then speak of who we had been in previous lifetimes. Simply knowing [the information] would have sufficed. Unfortunately, what you call jockeying for [acknowledgment and] position in our world was a common pursuit. And even when we did not participate in such activities, we were often accused of it anyway. [People tend to accuse others of their own wrongdoings (those of the accuser), yet another thing that has not changed throughout human history]. The absolute Truth here is that those who were conscious of the real value of this knowledge rarely spoke of it at all except most selectively, only in the most private way, and to only the most trusted companions. And so, although each lifetime is unique, we often may encounter similar circumstances, roles, or accompanying personalities to walk through one or more lifetimes with us. We may be of a different sex than we were in other lifetimes, have a different profession, or seem to have an outwardly different personality. The outer circumstances may be eerily similar to

---

[65] Refer to *The Book of Visions* for a summary of R. Hayyim Vital's spiritual lineage.

other lifetimes or wildly different, but one thing that does not vary is the essential nature of the Soul Root.

(To be continued)

December 10, 2019

If one is aggressive in nature and driven by ego and arrogance, that will be at the base of the human's being and actions throughout their incarnated lifetime. Those qualities may become tempered [to varying degrees] after the soul makes corrections as it learns through its various incarnated experiences — or, if the lessons are not learned, it may stay the same and cause itself the same difficulties lifetime after lifetime. Those essential qualities will not be eradicated as the core nature of the soul, but learning can temper those characteristics and contribute to the soul's evolution. Opportunities are presented during lifetimes to remediate various aspects that lead to the growth of the person and the greater soul.

Alternately, through Free Will, the personality of the individual incarnations may choose to negate the soul's learning and evolution. In the same vein, if the Soul Root's characteristics are, instead, of an innocent and trusting nature [or any other nature], the process and potential evolution [or devolution] are the same. A Soul Root determines the essential nature of each incarnated being/soul powered by that Soul Root. It continues [evolved or not] throughout the various incarnations. It does not follow a genealogical, but rather a soul line. [Since the Soul Root can be incarnated in a variety of timelines and circumstances, the actual evolution of that Soul Root is not necessarily linear (sequential) in nature.] The incarnations can materialize in any person regardless of their geographic location or genealogical lineage, but they will usually follow a [general] pathway created for them.

The Oversoul is made up of the Soul Roots and their fragments, along with their various personalities and experiences. The Oversoul is the composite of all the substance of Soul Roots and their essences [essential natures] and experiences. The Soul Roots return to the "mothership" [certainly not in any three-dimensional sense of the term] of the Oversoul to rest, recharge, and receive nourishment — to become, once again, part of the whole. Each of the Soul Roots delivers its cargo to the bodies that the soul will inhabit, and when it has discharged its cargo, it takes on the parts of itself that no longer have use for a physical body [at the point of physical death]. With those energies, it returns to the Oversoul for its recharge. Each Soul Root also deposits into the Oversoul the sum of the experiences of those they have brought from the physical world[s].

The Oversoul consists of the sum of its parts. It is, in essence, a processing center, a recharging station, and a home for the Soul Roots.

December 15, 2019

Yes, you are now reading a book about how one achieves the status of a saint or legend. Its author is attempting to explain accounts of the times, both by the subject himself and those in his orbit. And so, please consider how you are receiving this information. This is a source unaccounted for by the author of the article and by most researchers. Even a firsthand account has been marred by human perspective. A person's heart, mind, and eyes can only record with their own limited feelings, thoughts, and vision. Those things are regulated by the human limitations under which they operate. I, for example, knew what was in HaAri's heart and mind only to the extent my own heart and mind could comprehend. Although often merged with my own, his thoughts went far beyond what I could ever fathom because he had a depth of knowledge I could neither imagine nor access. And although we were almost constantly in each other's company during his time in Safed, even I did not hear his every word nor see his every action. So now imagine how much less the others knew of him.[66]

When we see someone perform an act, voice a prayer, or give a teaching, we cannot begin to imagine what triggered the action, the depth of knowledge behind it, or the true motivation behind it. Although there may appear to be an external trigger for the action, the internal causes are hidden from any other living being. We can merely witness and interpret through our own hearts, minds, and perceptions. We may think that we know, but we cannot truly know. And yet we speak as if we do know. We give our own words of explanation to it and present it as the only Truth

---

[66] Shivhei Ha'Ari – The legends and stories contained in the book are mainly based on the letters sent by Shlomo Meinsterl at the beginning of the seventeenth century from Palestine abroad. In these letters, Meinsterl related what he had heard of the greatness of the Ari. At first, the letters were published together with other books, but later different editors added new stories, and they appeared as separate books. "It was the hagiographical portrait of Shivhei ha-'Ari that inscribed the epoch-changing figure of Isaac Luria into the folkloric imagination of subsequent generations."
See Eitan P. Fishbane, "Perceptions of Greatness: Constructions of the Holy Man Shivhei ha-Ari," *Kabbalah: Journal for the Study of Jewish Mystical Texts*, Vol. 27, Los Angeles 2012, pp. 195-221, accessed December 26, 2022, https://www.academia.edu/16574626/Perceptions_of_Greatness_Constructions_of_the_Holy_Man_in_Shiv%E1%B8%A5ei_ha_Ari

of the situation. When we relate it to others, they also can only interpret it from their limited understanding. And I will go as far as to say that even the one who performs the action, voices the prayer, and teaches the teaching is not aware of the whole Truth of the matter because so often there is a level of Divine spirit involved that the actor himself may not even be aware of.

So, all we have remaining to pass on to history and succeeding generations is the sum of the reports and reflections of the observers and the observed; all of them are biased, skewed, and limited in some way. We hear what we need to hear, think what we need to think, and see what we need to see. We cannot hear, think, feel, or see according to the other's need [or perspective]. This Truth has been pervasive throughout time and history. In your time, you see glaring examples of this so that you may allow for making corrections in your process of *Tikkun*, or reparation. When this aspect [the glaring division of perspectives] of life arises so powerfully that it cannot be ignored for another moment, it is time to remove the blinders and come together in the understanding I just put forth (or expect serious breakage and damage to systems and the world).

At first glance, our differing reports and perspectives seem divisive for the purpose of destruction and chaos, but there exists, within the dissonance, a very high potential for healing. In bringing these differences to the surface of our communal consciousness, we have the potential to recognize and overcome them. We shall see what your world does with this information, as it is at one of these points of determination of what is to come. There are those who seem awakened yet follow blindly. There are those who seem to follow blindly but, in fact, have a complete understanding of the matter [from their perspective] and have consciously chosen this as their Truth. In the end, compassion and coming together to recognize and acknowledge the variance in perspectives that differentiate our views and opinions is imperative. If we comprehend that, yet another level of understanding can be created that draws all of us closer to the actual Truth.

Of course, human perspective can change according to the circumstances at the time of the perception's origin. Perhaps the perspective may also change if circumstances change sufficiently and new facts and understandings come to light. But what if the new perspective is not acknowledged, noted, and recorded?[67] Then, history is left with only the first opinion and recording of the Truth as seen without the increased value and information of the new perspective. There remains hope of a more truthful reckoning of some events and Truths, as they have shifted for me since their origins' time, place, and circumstances. [Simply put, I see things differently now and would like to note this fact. This is what sparked my communications with you.]

December 22, 2019

We have so much to discuss about the material you are now reading [*The Book of Visions*]. You are making discoveries about me and my life through my own words and thoughts when I had

---

[67] In the sacred text of the Talmud, laws are recorded as well as full discussions, arguments, and perspectives on those laws that were noted, considered, and recorded over centuries of input from a variety of scholars in a variety of geographical locations. Tradition demands respect and the value of a broad range of perspectives on a topic.

THE SOUL ROOT AND THE OVERSOUL

only the perspective of that lifetime. You wonder why I have spoken to you referring to Isaac Luria as HaAri rather than Ashkenazi, as I did in my lifetime. I often say things to you in ways you can better relate to rather than raise unnecessary questions. It is best you are comfortable as my thoughts flow through you and you form them into words. These small adjustments are of little consequence to me as my main goal is to be understood by you and anyone who will read what we are writing. It is enough that some of the concepts will be heady or strange, so your comfort level is important to me, or else you will not continue with the work.

It is also important you do not receive all the facts of my life and others all at once. There is much to assimilate and many surprises. It cannot and should not be done all at once. In fact, it was important you had come to this point in your life and learned all that you have learned before being able to transcribe this book and assimilate the information that has come to you already (as well as what is to come). I told you several times about what happened to me from getting too much learning too soon and too fast. I do not wish to inflict this kind of inundation upon you.

Yes, you are now realizing that your development has been orchestrated for you to enter new levels of understanding as appropriate for you and none too soon in your life. Your knowledge and your maturity have generally been matched so that you can assimilate [and integrate] the understanding without leaving you broken. You remember times in your life when you were almost broken by the disparity between your internal knowledge and the reality of where you found yourself. Now that you have come to a place of happiness and freedom, you are ready to receive more and more. Much of it will come from our association and our work together. You must receive and carry this information, and therefore, I have not pushed it to you until you become ready.

As for the information received by others, they will take in what is appropriate for them and only what will be helpful and informative to their lives. You must know that much of what you are learning and are about to learn may only apply to you and perhaps a few others. Still, you should know it will assist you in putting together mysteries of your life and your history through time. You have already noted this. Many are putting out important and essential teachings now, each in their own way, so that more and more people will become more aware and conscious about themselves and the world at this momentous time in the evolution of life on this planet.

December 24, 2019

So, you want to know what this Oversoul and Soul Root business has to do with everyday life and what benefit it is to know this kind of information. The level to which this knowledge is pursued depends on many factors, but for those who "read" other humans — reading them to help them, that is — it can be quite useful to know and, in turn, you can transmit the appropriate information to the subject. [All of this was something HaAri knew by just looking at a person.]

There are not so many in the world who wish to pursue the knowledge of others their Soul Root has inhabited [or perhaps in some circles there are], but knowing the essence of who you are in your core, without the influence of your circumstances, can be quite helpful. For some, their core essence can be seen by one and all. They wear it on the outside for all to observe. But for others, their core essence can be hidden under layers of the influences of environment, culture, family, etc. There are so many who wonder who they really are and what their purpose is for being in this world. Knowing about the Soul Root can be very helpful for such a person. It is important to remember that all of a person's existence is built upon this core essence, and the lessons to be learned and mastered through time are based upon it. It is again the question of, "Who are *you*, REALLY?"

Within this Soul Root are the building blocks of each lifetime. Most build structures around themselves. Some structures are sturdy and strong, hiding the essence of a person. But if things go well [in the development of the person], some blocks crumble, and windows open into the essence that was being hidden by the false nature of the blocks, the "I" of the ego. With some work and a strong sense of self, the wall will come down [usually bit by bit, but sometimes it can happen all at once] and free the person's soul essence, the Root, so it can be seen. This allows the person to function at their highest level, enabling them to see their purpose and how to fulfill it.

I will tell you that despite the fact that the core of all life is a seed coming from the Source of All Creation, which is only Love, a shell surrounds that seed. The shell is the source of the Soul Root. From it grows the various character traits that transmit the essence of the Soul Root. Now, each manifestation of the Soul Root exhibits these traits to one degree or another. That is to say that the Soul Root does not only belong to one person, but rather exists in fragments that are allowed to be shared by different people, some of whom may exist in the same timeline.

INSPIRATION AND IMPERMANENCE

December 26, 2019

From the Transcriber
Note: *The following paraphrases the original text, which was lost due to a technical issue.*

I sat down to write and again realized that most inspirations are not my own. Only the choice to act upon the inspirations is mine. I had a vivid vision of a guided meditation from almost 30 years ago. Our meditation group was led to a beach with the understanding we would receive a gift. When I looked down the beach, I saw an enormous golden Light in the shape of a human — and it was headed toward me.

We were face-to-face when the Light somehow broadcast a message to me that I will not forget: "I have no face. You have a face and can do (will do?) on Earth that which I cannot." And at that moment, a great heat and high vibration were delivered into my hands that did not abate for months. Others could feel the energy at a distance of one to two feet away from my hands. The energy was directed toward those who needed healing.

This occurred somewhere between 1986 and 1990. To this day, my hands begin to vibrate and become hot when I am in the presence of someone who might benefit from healing.

At first, I thought the Light was God, then years later, I thought it was the Golden Ones,[68] and when I sat down to write this work, I considered it might have been "Hayyim."

Revelations come slowly but consistently. And just when we think "the information" has come to Light, we are bestowed with new information that turns the previous information and understanding on its head.

---

[68] An ancient source of souls that inhabit this Earth and other realms.

THE SECRET OF LIFE

January 23, 2020

My dear girl, do you think my life was spent with each day reaching a high level of measurable productivity? No, of course not. What you must know is something you already know and, therefore, only have to recall. As one who channels the Light and maintains a conscious connection with the Source of All, you know this comes at a cost to the human. The greater mission is lived by moving forward with the soul's development and growth, by living in the Light, and by bringing it forward to assist others. It matters not to how many, for there may be but only one to whom a person delivers the sacred Light (but that is doubtful). That one is the one designated to be touched by you and by what you have to offer. If there is more than one, that is delightful. But if there is only one, then that is also delightful and is cause for celebration.

    What I want to tell you is that not each and every day is lived at top speed, at maximum capacity, as so many are made to believe. Rather, it is lived at the capacity of what you have available to give each day. Each person varies in their reserve of energy and their strength of momentum. You have many days that you label as non-productive. What you do not see is the fullness of each moment — whether or not you are the one who fills it.

You see me as one who was prolific in my teachings and writings and the various other work I did in my time. I accomplished all that in spurts of concentrated effort and even during some hyperactive episodes. I spent much time without measurable achievement, embroiled in chaotic and misaligned relationships, in squabbles (both internal and external), contemplation, and awaiting my muse and advisors before I could move forward. Some of this time was productive, and some destructive. I did not see the value of any of that time, but it was indeed valuable. We need not only to live out a mission, but rather live a life with all the experiences necessary to develop our personality, character, and soul. Nothing is a waste of time unless we deem it so. All the time you spend to feed your soul is necessary, and all the time you spend avoiding what you feel that you must do is also necessary. When you spend time doing the things that take you away from that which you also want to do, you find out what is important to you more effectively than if you did only that one thing and became enslaved to it, unaware of other pursuits.

Decide what you want to do — nothing is a bad choice if it leads you to better choices on other days. All your pursuits are valuable and aid in your growth. I cannot tell you of the days that I agonized in nothingness, the nothingness of non-activity, of not connecting with others, of solitary confinement of my creation, and in grief. One day, I may call it meditation or contemplation, and another, I may call it morosely looking out a window. It is, as you say, all in how you look at something. I did not have the perspective or peace of mind much of the time, so I was hard on myself during those seemingly non-productive times. I am telling you from my new perspective that all *is well*, and we cannot always be swimming laps. Sometimes, we can just tread water, stand in the pool, or look at the water from a distance. It is all valuable. We each have different ways of recharging and affecting our own growth. Some like to win the race, some like to swim laps, and some delight in simply being in the water.

Whatever you decide to do, delight in it. Whatever you decide to do, delight in it. *That, my dear, is the secret of life.* That is the secret that so many lust after and hurt themselves trying to find out. That is the secret that so many will never learn. Even if it is doing nothing at all, delight in those moments, and you will be happy and fulfill your mission on Earth.

BRING IT ALL TOGETHER

January 24, 2020

This is a process you see. The writing of this book serves not only to convey its material to others but also includes your connection, education, and maturation process. For the information to come to a person all at once, before they are prepared to receive it, would [to some degree] perpetuate the same difficulty that I had in my own life of not being emotionally prepared and mature enough to integrate the text learning, the deep Wisdom, and real-life skills in a balanced fashion. It caused me no end of misery. We do not want that for anyone.

You now realize that much was to be experienced by you before you could even begin to take on this project. The seed for this project was planted before you came into this world, and we checked in from time to time during your life to assess your readiness. At times, we began the transmission but then determined that the time was not quite right to continue. Currently, you are ready to accept the material and make sure that it gets out to the world without compromising your personal well-being. This is a lifetime of integration for you, a lifetime of learning balance, and, for this reason, you have not been pushed to do things before your time. For some, the life trajectory is about other things, and each learns what they need in their own way. When you teach the lessons (and this will happen in the not-too-distant future), you will attract those who are ready and open to the materials and techniques, as this is essential to the teachings and as evidenced by the life of Isaac Luria. All of his life was preparation for his arrival in Safed, where he was ready for the community, and the community was not only open to him but was the place where he would come to full bloom. You must live first that which you will put forth to others. If your life does not have integrity by the way you walk through it and by what you teach, it simply will not be a viable course for you, others, or Truth. We, and you, have put forth too much effort not to have this work come into a printed form of communication.

It is incumbent upon all humans on the planet at this time who have available to them the teaching of Truth and conscious connection to the Light and Love in the Universe to make their knowledge available to others. Truth and connection take many forms, so teach and demonstrate in a variety of ways so that a variety of people may be open to the teachings. You have only to decide that *YOU are ready to share.*

KNOWING

January 25, 2020

And now, about that which you have been reading from my *Book of Visions,* the journey of my soul as revealed to me by HaAri. I revealed on those pages many details that are not always easy to follow [especially without full knowledge of the history of our sages]. But before discussing with you the explanations of the levels of the soul and the ways in which they manifest themselves in humans, I want to make a greater point that deals with only those specific details of what I wrote. Among the overwhelming number of details I give in my writings is an insight into the nature and brilliance of HaAri. I have spoken many times of his loving nature and the Light that he brought [and still brings] to the world. It all seemed simple and uncomplicated for him as he walked through his life, giving hope and healing, information and revelations, and compassion to all, including his students. If he met a man or woman in the street, he could converse in a most uncomplicated fashion. He communicated in simple words about the simple things in life. The more one studied with him and knew him, the more one was drawn into the layers beneath his outward façade of utter simplicity. To use the word façade does not imply that this was a false persona that he wore in the world. On the contrary, this simplicity was indeed his very essence. Only by one's understanding of the world and readiness to accept greater understandings of life and God and the greater Universe did the layers begin to lift off him, revealing new depth within each of his words. How did he know all that he did? I have to say that he felt he knew everything and nothing at the same time. The information he shared depended on a person's receptivity and ability to integrate it. Somehow, he always knew. He exuded confidence that indicated he would know all that was needed in any given moment or circumstance. Yet, it was not his to hold onto. It was only there [within him] when he needed to give the information to others [for their benefit].

———◆———

So, as far as what was revealed to me by my teacher and all the myriad details, one would never believe that he was a vessel for this degree of knowledge. I understand that one may wonder about the use of having all this knowledge. And how did he hold all of this? I believe that access to this knowledge came to him as needed, and in his case, the pitcher of water from the well was set before him, whereas most of us have to go to the well to draw up the water. But first, we have to locate the well. There are many analogies that I am tempted to continue with here, but I believe I have made my point.

Concerning lineage and *gilgul* [reincarnation]: Was it important for me to have the details of who I had been in the past and who co-inhabited my body [*ibbur*] at the time? I thought so, both before and as he relayed the information to me. To ensure my understanding — for it was not simply idle chatter or random facts. He explained this to me contextually, in language I could understand. He conveyed it to me in a way that made it matter to me at the time and elevated my consciousness to a level commensurate with what he had described. But to be honest, I never fully comprehended. How could I, since all the contextual knowledge of man is but of his own construct? He revealed all of this to me in my own language that I could integrate into my life as best I could.

January 26, 2020

I previously mentioned that it was an ongoing conversation amongst those in our circle to speak of our spiritual lineage. I also said that it was very easy to allow one's ego to become too involved with knowledge of these facts. Some sought gravitas in the community with their claims of lineage, be they true or merely perceived. Some inflated their importance with the knowledge, and there was pressure to "be somebody," not just in the present but throughout time. This was destructive to the core fabric of what we were about, to be honest, and most likely the reason that HaAri was reluctant to tell me of all the transmigrations and the *ibburim* that I had and would experience again. This all led to a greater understanding of myself, and yet, what was one to do with the information? To expound upon it to others would be an act of ego, but to not integrate it into my inner being would be to reject the holy gift of this knowledge.

Since we lived in a world where great honor was given to the sages and those who wrote and interpreted our people's laws and customs, if we connected with them, we would naturally (and understandably) conflate our stature and importance with theirs.

Yet this was indeed *not* the point of receiving this information. In my case, I was given the information so that I would have an explanation for some of the interests, "peculiarities," and events of my life. It was to help me understand myself and some of that which had befuddled me about my life choices. It offered reasonable explanations for what I did or did not study, my particular interests in life, relationships, and some of the choices I made on my life path. It helped me to understand my life.

BOUND BY FEAR

January 28, 2020

When and where we come into being in the world determines our boundaries. I speak of the earthly boundaries that are created through the fears and limitations that are formed by the human mind in the third dimension. These unreasonable boundaries of fear and misunderstood universal principles prevent humans from fulfilling their divine missions and from growth that would advance their development in a much more accelerated manner. You have the current political situation on your mind, and so I will tell you that it is a perfect example of what I am teaching at this very moment. All chaos is borne of fear, and it is borne of those limitations that I just mentioned. The chaos comes from fear of losing position, losing hope, being wrong, being shamed, being discovered to be acting beyond your knowledge or abilities, being less than others, losing what you worked for or what was given in life, and losing faith in the universal order. There are more fears, of course, but we begin with these. The limitations concern who may achieve what in life, the level to which they may rise, the level at which their creativity may be allowed to flourish, and the extent to which they may express themselves freely. Unfortunately, the list, if complete, would be very long.

January 29, 2020

And so, we begin where we left off yesterday. Your time in history is not so new as it is a repetition of base human tendencies now elevated to a high and widespread degree and level due to the urgency of the need for course correction. Urgency always demands more of a person, a family, a culture, and a society. There are times of relative tranquility in the world, and there are times of obvious crisis, usually due to the apparentness of the tranquility that preceded it. You see, the human being is capable of complacency almost more than any other state of being. Rumblings of discontent (both individual and communal) go unheard or dismissed until the pressure builds and erupts, creating discord and chaos and the hopeful expectation of change. This condition exists both in the Light of life and the Darkness of life.

Why is it that discontent desires to outweigh joy and happiness? Why is the path to joy and happiness interfered with by those in a state of discontent? When a path of Light is set forth, there are always those who feel that it is incumbent upon them to redirect, rebuke, or otherwise disrupt those who have found their way to that path. What compels so many to try to obliterate the happiness that others feel, as well as the path they follow to find it? These are age-old questions. As in my time and place in history, so many seek to discredit those of us who are charting a new course — not a completely new course, but innovative and divergent enough from the well-worn path to rile them up and present a threat to them (in their own minds only).

January 30, 2020

There is much to say today concerning the words that you have read from my *Book of Visions*. You read about the source of my soul, of transmigrations and details, and of the lineages and the sins and the reparations for sins that were both mine and not mine [at the time, both known and unknown]. And you read of the ways I was to do the work to atone for and repair or correct these sins [both mine and those of the other aspects of the souls that attached themselves to me].

When I asked HaAri to reveal to me the details of my soul and its travels through this world, I was not expecting what he told me. I was expecting more than a fairy tale, but the substance of what he said was beyond my comprehension. The details and convolutions of the passage of souls from one life to the next (and into MY life) and the details of what they carried with them were overwhelming. How could all of this have been within me without my awareness? Would I have lived or experienced life differently at the time if I had known that these things were being presented to me in life with the potential that my choices would be of such consequence? To be honest, I do not know when I would have been ready for all this information, but I did request it with unrelenting insistence. To be honest, much of what he told me about the transmigration of other souls into my person and my failure to perform the corrections for them when presented with the opportunities deeply saddened me and left me feeling quite guilty and heavy-hearted. I cannot help but think that he told me as much as he did because he knew that he would not be able to do so in the future, for he left this world not too long after he revealed the information to me.[69]

I was overwhelmed by the quantity of souls and the accompanying details with which my own soul was bound. Now, you may ask about the importance of the detailed information I was given. Once again, I repeat that the information was a product of the times, religion, and culture. Our frame of reference dictated the details and extent of the revelation. Not only was everyone in our circle occupied with these matters, but some of us saw what we were given as a way to purify ourselves — and hence repair ourselves in a way that would help correct and repair the whole world.

Needless to say, in my state of being and maturity at that stage of my life (I was 29 when HaAri entered into my life), it was impossible for me to comprehend or digest the quantity and depth of information given to me and the many protocols[70] prescribed (as stated in *Sefer Hahezyanot*).

---

[69] And yet he did reveal more in his *Book of Visions*.
[70] Ways to achieve *Tikkun* and remediation.

SUFFERING AND RESTRICTION

January 31, 2020

It was within the general mindset of our time that suffering and restriction were a sure path to the Divine, to holiness. [So much so that we very often overlooked the joy commanded of us.[71]] This was the reason for the myriad of details of the protocols that were assigned to me to make the necessary corrections to my soul and the souls that dwelled within me through *gilgul* [reincarnation] and *ibbur* [impregnation or walk-in]. We also believed that Love was a way to the Divine, but I now hold that only the latter of these paths is the correct and effective one.

Suffering and ascetic restriction only lead to more suffering and restriction in the opposite direction of Joy. Yet it is what we did and how we lived was a result of the times [and the place] in which we lived. From my current perspective, I would say that all of it was necessary to fulfill the needs of the era, but I would not choose to live that way again. It was, as with so many of our practices, a result of the general surroundings and our culture.

---

[71] When man faces his Maker, he shall give a reckoning for the joys of life that he failed to experience. Talmud Yerushali.

Since the beginning, much of our Jewish practice and observance have been keyed into the local culture to draw in our people and assimilate into the surrounding culture while preserving our unique cultural and religious identity. Prevailing winds have always drawn us in, in every time and every place we have ever lived.

Many people today live with the same suffering and deprivation that we chose back then, but more often than not, they do not choose it as intentionally as we did. The rigors of religious asceticism do not create a more holy human. I say with certainty that living [and behaving] in a state of unconditional Love will always lead a person to the right behavior and the actual *Tikkun* [repair] the world needs. Only in Love are these true and lasting corrections made. Doing violence to oneself by imposing the sometimes-severe ascetic standards [of self or society] does not help anyone. That is what it is, violence to the pure and loving natural nature of the original soul.

THE BOOK OF VISIONS

February 3, 2020[72]

My dear, just because one is given comprehension or enlightenment does not mean that life is all sparkles and dancing down a clear path. There are always obstacles along that path; there are troubles to be encountered and dealt with. It is how we deal with the challenges and obstacles that determines our degree of enlightenment. Rejection or acceptance of the sparks with which one has been gifted is evident in the way that one deals with the challenges of life. There would be no need for such enlightenment if there were nothing on the path to challenge you and, indeed, for you to shed light upon.

It is all about the choices we make when faced with each challenge that determines our level of ascension [for lack of a better word]. If we see a man in the street who is in need, do we scorn him? Do we look upon him with pity? Do we notice him at all? And if we notice him, do we assume we can do nothing to improve his life and pass him by? Do we give him a few coins or a piece of bread and keep walking? Do we sit beside him, offer him

---

[72] This transmission corroborates what appears in R. Hayyim's *Sefer HaHezyanot* (*The Book of Visions*).

a smile and some words, and listen to his story? Do we take him home and feed him — maybe clothe him? There are so many ways to respond to any person or situation. Our degree of enlightenment does not show itself through exhaustive study and reverence by the minions. It shows itself in how we respond to other humans, situations, and the world.

When I was told that I should live in Jerusalem and that it was there that I would find my essence, spiritual home, and self-understanding, I expected that this would bring great peace to my spirit and my being. It brought me confusion and left me unsure of myself and what I was to do, even given my position in Jewish society and the legal system there. This is often how it is, for even having studied and learned the lessons taught to me from the lofty heights of the knowledge of HaAri himself, I did always remain cognizant that in every cell of my being, my well-being would be determined by my personal connection with the Light, which was within me, and that that very connection was what would lead to my total comprehension. Instead, it often lay dormant within me, within my intellect, and did not connect with my heart — and that, my dear, is all of it. That, my dear, is the secret that is not a secret.

Connect the knowledge of the intellect with the heart, and then the soul comes alive. Knowledge without heart is never the path to enlightenment. Wisdom and Understanding are above Knowledge — yes, they are all connected, but Wisdom and Understanding are at a higher level in the order of things.[73] Wisdom, Knowledge, and Understanding must give way to action.

---

[73] See "The Kabbalistic Tree of Life" in the Appendix.

As I have mentioned, it is an *avayra* (sin) not to bring these things into the physical world with action.[74]

Often, and sadly, knowledge has been given elevated status, above and to the exclusion of Wisdom and Understanding. I did not learn in my heart that true Wisdom and enlightenment are states of joy and compassion undeterred by that which we encounter along the way. Ah, it is exactly the challenges along the way, the bumps in the road, and our responses to them that determine our level of ascension. It did not matter how learned I was; due to various aspects of my personality, I did not integrate enough joy or compassion into my life. It was dealing with people that always did me in. It was as though those skills eluded me for the length of my days. I, too often, succumbed to the influence of other's opinions of me, be they positive or negative. This sometimes resulted in false bravado, arrogance and anger, and a general inability to, as you would say, play well with others. I did not understand how a person like me could contain the elevated soul that my teacher revealed to me. He also tried to ingrain in me that we are not what we seem to be. "Man sees only what is visible, but the Lord sees into the heart."[75]

Know that the greatness of the soul does not depend on the person's deeds but is according to the times and his generation since a very significant deed in a generation like this is equivalent

---

[74] "Anyone whose good deeds exceed his wisdom, his wisdom will endure. And anyone whose wisdom exceeds his good deeds, his wisdom will not endure." Pirke Avot (Ethics of the Fathers), 3:12.

[75] Based on 1 Samuel, 16:7 and spoken by Isaac Luria to Hayyim Vital. See *The Book of Visions*, 5:8.

to several great deeds in other generations.[76] At the time, this led me to believe, once again, that I was special and apart and once more fed my arrogance. Alas, this was a (if not *the*) great wrestling match of my life. I struggled with others, but most of all, I struggled within myself. I was lauded by my elders, whom I respected, for my knowledge and what was perceived to be the luminescence of my soul, yet I knew myself to be easily influenced by the words and moods of others, that my temperament left much to be desired, and I was always hoping for more than I had — in all regards. And I did make many life decisions that were to my detriment. This is quite a public admission from me; I am not sure that I saw it all at the time I lived that life. I did not consciously see it, but I had the sense of it and was unsettled by my struggle within. I may have seen it more clearly when elevated to a higher plane in meditation, perhaps. I certainly did not see it as clearly as I do from my present perspective and as I give you these words. It is rare for anyone to see themselves with clarity while living in the physical world, still in the body and in the thick of what some describe as "the density of the third dimension."

My teacher HaAri showed me this, with all the knowledge of these things that I have just described to you, and I said to him that I understood, but many of my attributes were difficult, too difficult to face. But these were the challenges of my life, essential to my learning as much as the texts I studied with such vigor and commitment. The texts are of little value without the humanity to accompany them. I wanted to be more than I was and did not know how to do this. I wanted to be a better husband and father,

---

[76] Vital, *The Book of Visions*, 5:7.

a better teacher, a better colleague, and a better human. I did not really, or perhaps fully, understand why I had difficulty communicating with others. Look at all that I wrote. Look at all that I preached and taught. And somehow, I felt that I did not know how to speak with people in general, so I wrote.

When HaAri came into my physical life for that brief time, I found myself finally understood by someone, finally able to communicate on a level that surpassed anything that had been before. And now, I can say it surpassed any communication that took place for the duration of my long life. Yes, he came to me often (in spirit), with the exception of some "blackout" periods from time to time, which I explain in *The Book of Visions*, but our connection was never the same. Sometimes (many times), my inner isolation and solitude were both refuge and torture for me. To be dropped again into the world of not truly being understood after he left this world was almost too much for me.

Sometimes, we all need human understanding. The same way that someone sending you loving thoughts is never the same as getting an actual physical hug.

Anyway, I rarely felt understood or appreciated, and often, I stood at both ends of the spectrum at the same time. What I mean by that is that I felt inferior and superior at the same time. Throughout my life, I was told of my genius for texts and the lofty lineage of my soul, but I was also told and accused of misaligned motives, an overinflated ego, and an overly proprietary attitude concerning the Lurianic legacy. Praise and criticism had an equally strong effect on me. It seemed to me that I could not please anyone for more than a moment at a time, least of all myself. I convinced myself many times that I was above the others, which is why they misunderstood me and maligned me, never accepting that my actions and comportment created this response in others.

THE WONDER AND MARVEL OF CREATION

February 5, 2020

So, this is where we meet today [Lake Meade National Park in Nevada], away from all [intense, heavy] vibrational density, people, and their constructions, both physical and non-physical. This space is essential for the soul to retreat from the creations of man. It is essential to step away from the heavy influences that surround us, no matter how well-intentioned they may be. There are times for physical interaction and for being in a place that is alive with activity and the constructions of what man has built for himself. But more often than is convenient, people who live in densely populated areas must extract themselves from the dense vibration and retreat to a place of nature where they can breathe — to a place where every in-breath marvels at the creation around it, whether the creation is a blade of grass, a rock, a leaf on a tree, majestic mountains, or a body of water. At the proper time [and when we are focused], all these creations remind us of Source and encourage us to join and engage with all of Source's creations.

The wonder and marvel of Creation can become lost in everyday life and living in a societal and architectural structure.

The loss oppresses our soul, which wishes to breathe in the open air and the glory of nature's wonder surrounding us. This is where we need to be when we go inward to connect with Source. Yes, we can go inward wherever we are, anywhere, but ahh, to be in the open, in nature, to see nothing but the creations of Source and none of the creations of man. This is what activates our very cells; it activates our vibration. Being in undisturbed nature, where all is clean, free, and "uncorrected," raises our vibration. We can take in the majesty of the Source's creations in nature. This was behind the idea of going into the field to welcome the Sabbath just before sundown. Yes, the Sabbath can be welcomed anywhere and still enter the heart and mind, but there is an added dimension and grandeur to welcome her out in nature, away from man's constructs.

I want to remind you to do this more often. I want to remind you not to get caught up in the creations of man alone. Meditate on and disappear into the leaves of a plant, a blade of grass, or a tree if you do not have the time or the ability to get to a place like I describe or to another isolated spot in nature. Look out a window and, if you see a tree, fly to it in your mind. Sit in the tree and enjoy the view. Be at one with that creation and know that the power of such contact can help restore you. Too many times, we forget. We forget about its power until we again find ourselves out in nature. Then it comes back to us: we are reminded and held close by Source. Being in and appreciating the natural environment, free of human thought and creations, is where the spirit soars and the connection is complete and direct. This is why I wanted to join you here today. You know I can meet with you anywhere, but today I wanted to experience this here with you. Be still. Please take it in. Be at one with your Source. You are needed.

April 4, 2020

From the Transcriber

I received this transmission after the start of the Covid-19 pandemic.

=======◆=======

What you are now going through in the world is magnified due to the greatly increased size of your population and the urgent need for paradigm changes. As you know, in my day, the plague took our master from us, including our master HaAri at a young age. Sadly, it was time for him to leave for reasons I may have discussed earlier.[77]

---

[77] This topic also arises in *The Book of Visions*, but It is not a topic upon which R. Hayyim wishes to dwell.

MESSAGES

April 23, 2020

You have heard me speak many times of the Unifications[78] that were so much a part of our practice. There was a high degree of ritualization in our day, and you know there is a high degree of ritualization common to most religions. Ritualization was originally a way to supply guidance but eventually developed into a way to restrict and control followers. The rituals that I speak of regarding the act or process of Unification were ritualistic and stringent but were *not meant to control the masses*; they were safety measures to preserve and elevate the well-being of the person on our path. As one would enter unknown worlds between this life and the One, it was necessary to have the road map that I discussed at length and have precautions in place for a safe journey. This is a journey to be undertaken with great care and supervision under all circumstances.\

---

[78] There were prescriptions and formulas for achieving Unification with the Divine (*Yichud*). Some were general and some were specific for a certain level of Unification that was necessary for a particular circumstance or condition. To a lesser degree, Unifications were also directed to communicate with a departed soul, so as to connect with their wisdom.

I was guided on my Unification journeys for a time by my beloved teacher, Arizal,[79] and Elijah himself. In the practice of these processes, sometimes I heard messages prompted by the various citations and permutations of the letters I uttered.[80] At times, the messages were clear, and at other times, they took a long time to develop and have meaning to me. It was a process not unlike the development of a photograph: the photo becomes more defined as it increasingly reveals its clarity through the process. Strategic markers appear along the journey of Unification, for if this were not true, no human could reach the destination and survive.[81]

Sometimes, the messages would appear at those markers, and sometimes they would not. Generally, the messages were encouraging and meant to strengthen me. They often suggested clues and answers that would be known to the most learned men and those who lived in the prescribed way of goodness and purity. Only some messages were outright encouraging. Most chastised me for neither following prescribed practices nor fulfilling specific promises I had made. I often fell back on my promises and, throughout my years, was instructed on the havoc of my own

---

[79] Arizal is a different way to speak of HaAri. It is a way of informing that the person being mentioned has died. When a person has died, whenever we mention his name, we add, *zichrona livracha* (May his memory be for a blessing). When we mention this in written form, we write (in English) the abbreviation, z"l. Therefore, Arizal, is Ari + z"l.

[80] Permutation (recombination) of the Hebrew letters (usually of God's holy name) is a technique of combining and recombining the letters for the purpose of meditation or contemplation that can lead to higher states of consciousness and awareness. This practice developed as part of the ecstatic experience. The Hebrew letters are a pathway to expanded and creative consciousness.

[81] See "Four Who Entered the Garden" in the Appendix.

making. It was made clear to me on many more than one occasion exactly what I had done — or did *not do* — to bring on certain situations in my life. This information appears on numerous pages in *The Book of Visions*. [I want to say that when messages chastise or rebuke, they are inevitably messages of one's creation (usually from the subconscious). Divine messages never chastise or rebuke but are compassionate and emanate only with Love.] In all honesty, I now know that these chastisements came through my inner filter of regret and disappointment in myself. Some of these things I could repair, and some I could not. I could change things in the future and, in that fashion, make repairs, but not everything could be amended. And, believe me, the guilt and remorse from knowing this is almost unbearable. They are quite agonizing and take a toll on a person. Here, I speak about myself. And on some level, I believed (then more so than now) I was meant to suffer for the times I missed opportunities to correct the mistakes of myself and others. Performing the Unifications, I felt, would help not only in the redemption of humanity and the Jews but also of myself.

It was not easy in my daily life or spiritual practice for myself or others. Some of the messages I heard were meant to appeal to my ego, which sometimes would push me forward in my efforts. But in truth, it is counterproductive to work from a place of ego, which is meant to be put aside in such holy efforts. This is spelled out in Part 4 of *The Book of Visions*. I wrote in such detail that some believed me mad. No one likes to be thought of as mad, especially when the material they are putting forth might be dismissed because of that. This belief persisted in the years that followed. Still, the detail was necessary at the time so that I could also explain myself to both me and my audience. In my day, we were dependent upon this overabundance of details. This was an extension of the way we lived our lives and the way we studied and practiced life in excruciating detail. And I was a master of detail, at least regarding my studies and writings.

CONSEQUENCE

April 24, 2020

I held on to whatever my teacher HaAri told me, as if his words had come directly from God. But I will tell you this: something inside me occasionally fought his words, just as I resisted him when he first came to Safed. Without him right in front of me, touching my heart, repeating the words, reinforcing my resolve, and giving me the hands-on experiences to back it all up, I lost the momentum and resolve to do exactly as I was instructed. And to be honest, even when he was with me and gave me precise instructions for a task, I sometimes thought I knew better and did not follow his exact instructions. He always knew that if the result was not as he had predicted, it was due to my not following his exact instructions. Yet I often persisted in taking steps away from the precise instructions despite knowing that he was correct in the precision of his directives. I was not always cognizant of just how precise the details were that I needed to attend to, and as a result, I strayed from them — and was always surprised at how things turned out.

People often discount how their actions contribute to a variance in the result predicted by another. For example, suppose you are told that if you do X, then Y will happen. But then, when you do X, Y does NOT happen. Does this mean that the prediction was wrong? Not necessarily. Perhaps it means that free will entered even though you did X. Perhaps you did it without the proper intention, or perhaps you also did Q, or S, or some other thing that was not factored into the original equation when the instruction was given. Attitude, intention, and the subconscious also enter into whether or not something predicted will come to pass as projected.

For example, at one point in my life, I was directed to go to Damascus to preach, teach, and spread the word and the practices that we developed in Safed. I was not successful there for a variety of reasons, but mainly because I still needed to fulfill my mission and resisted doing so. I was to have preached to the people about their sins and their need to repent.

I was to cause the people to repent, and I did not. I did not follow up on those who did repent. This was entirely out of my own dysfunction and, may I say, disorientation during that time. It seemed too much responsibility, and so I did not bear the yoke of it. [The trajectories of life shift or are cut off if you do not comply with your holy tasks — and you are not the only one to suffer. Too many paid the price for my faults and omissions. And I paid dearly as I was told that my daughter died due to my task being undone.][82]

I lost the will and intention with which I had gone there, and so I made choices that were not for my own good or the good of others. I failed miserably; I did not extend myself as I should have because I felt shunned. *I allowed my ego to interfere with my*

---

[82] Morris M. Faierstein, Translator, "Introduction," in Vital, *The Book of Visions*.

mission. No matter how beautifully a table is set or how delicious the food is, one still has the choice of whether or not to eat at that table. "If one is engaged to assist the spirit, it may be that it is also for the benefit of the one who assists."[83] I neither ate at that table in Damascus nor did I do a good job feeding the people there.

I was later instructed to go to Jerusalem, where the prediction was that I would succeed, and again, the table was beautifully set, and the food was well prepared, but I did not eat the full meal, nor did I enjoy that which I did eat. According to the words of HaAri, I would find my true self and my essence in Jerusalem. It was there that I would truly comprehend what was needed for me to know about myself and all else, the mysteries of the Universe! Although I achieved some stature as a judge, teacher, and preacher there, I knew that this was not my finest hour. My finest hour was not something I would ever achieve in my lifetime [in my mind], save for the time I spent in the physical company of HaAri and when I transcribed the teachings that returned my soul to the Divine. For if I had believed of myself what was believed by those whom I considered my true council in this life, I would have eaten that meal with gratitude and asked for more. Instead, I did not eat but asked for more anyway, which does not seem to make sense, but it is the nature of many. [Look, in the world of your day, people are always asking for more before they have finished chewing or digesting what they have before them.]

When told of my merit, I not only discounted but mocked it by not believing and living up to it. For all that I believed in the good in others, I garnered all my criticism upon myself rather than

---

[83] Vital, *The Book of Visions.*

others. Only half of that is admirable — to believe the best in others. This is part of the reason for my having made choices in life that were detrimental to myself and, as a result, at times, to the community at large. Sometimes, these choices resulted from a lack of ego and sometimes from too much ego. I did not believe the good press that came my way, so I made choices that would prove that what others said was wrong. [This is not an uncommon thing to do. Many throughout time have demonstrated this approach to not feeling worthy of the praise heaped upon them.]

For all my studies and my learning, in my mind, I never measured up to the accolades. I was painfully aware of this. And to prove all of it wrong, I repeatedly did things to prove that I was right and that they were wrong. My choice of wives, my family life, my choice of paths to follow, and my refusal to follow instructions that would benefit both me and the world were all caused by my deep lack of belief in what others saw in me. The issue of Free Will is not unique to me, and I write of it here so that others will take heed and clear their path to live their mission and destiny. Jonah[84] could not take on the duties assigned to him because of his lack of belief in himself. He was not lazy; he deeply did not believe himself capable of what was expected of him. Had he believed, no one else's doubts would have affected him; they would not have stopped him. If given too much credence, the doubt of one's abilities is the most lethal blow to success. Even if it appears to the outside world that you are achieving success, knowing what you know about yourself does not seem like success because you know what heights you can reach. And you do not arrive at that

---

[84] In The Book of Jonah, Jonah was called upon by God to prophesy the destruction of Nineveh but goes to great lengths to escape the Divine mission.

place of being successful in your mission because of what you feel about yourself. ***By not doing what you were meant to do, you cause harm to the world!*** And the same is true if you stand in the way of another's mission!

———◆———

As a child, I was caught between knowing I was just me, a child, and hearing what my elders had to say about me. I now believe I became stuck in that space and never found my way out of that situation. I was always finding some way to place stumbling blocks between my reality and the future others had predicted for me. It was only during my time with HaAri on Earth that I found balance and, in that balance, my security — balance and wings to take flight. But even when I had time with him, I sometimes allowed my ego and doubt to seep in. It was evident that I could not leave my ego behind with my incessant requests for knowledge that he was unwilling or unable to impart to me.

At this point, my life could have turned one way or another. I did not honor or understand his resolve not to reveal certain information but rather was insistent on the matter. Intellectually, I was able to understand and manage it (maybe not completely), but emotionally I was not ready. I could not leave well enough alone, and with the knowledge about the secrets of my soul, I became overloaded with information, fear, and responsibility. [I had no idea of the depth and complexity of what would be revealed to me. When I asked, he told me, "No," but I insisted over and over and over again. And even with his warnings, I persisted. Both of us would pay the price for his revelations. I had to live with it, and he died because of it: the betrayal of his promise not to reveal the information.[85] I was young when I heard this information, and I have to say I was riddled with guilt and shame at the knowledge that in many cases I had made things worse. I missed opportunities for *Tikkun* (repair), and I also committed my own sins.][86] It was not until later in my life that he revealed to me that the betrayal of his holy promise caused his death,[87] though others vaguely alluded to it during my lifetime. They did not know the exactitude of what happened, but they believed it to be caused by my actions.

This determined my trajectory for the rest of my life. I would have preferred a life of balance and wise choices, but it was not to be because I was overburdened with the knowledge I had gained. My grief at the passing of my teacher also caused me to make some poor personal choices. How could he have left me when it was he who stood as a buffer between me and the world? How could he have left me with those who did not understand what truly gave Light to his words and true teachings? I devoted the rest of my life to writing his words and transmitting his ideas, but I did not follow his personal directives to me. I know it does not quite make sense. Maybe it was because I saw the distance between who and what he was and who and what I was. Nothing about me measured up to him (in my mind), so I felt I could only succeed by presenting his words and thoughts — in print. My lack of skills with people frightened me enough not to believe I might

---

[85] Various sources state that it was because of the revelation to Hayyim that Luria died. He had made a holy promise not to reveal the information and when he betrayed that promise, knowing that he would die if he did. He did it anyway.
[86] Vital, *The Book of Visions*, 4:8.
[87] Detailed in Vital, *The Book of Visions*.

have the desired effect with the spoken word. And so, I refused to believe I could have the desired effect with my words and influence on the people of Damascus.

ON WOMEN

May 14, 2020

I will supply you with the information you would like about the role of women in our society and our circle. It is true that my personal relationships with women were, in general, somewhat less than ideal — worse than my relationships with other men and people in general. This was due to personal ineptitude rather than any diminution of women on my part. There were those whom I held in high esteem. But you ask because you have been reading about the role of women as spiritual leaders and authorities[88] and know a great deal about what was happening in my day and previous centuries. You also have knowledge of some of the women in my community, which factors into what you receive from your reading.

The general knowledge of the times assumes the inferior role of women in the religious and spiritual community. This is only somewhat true. There were both greater and lesser exceptions to this assumption. Many women had abilities and insights that

---

[88] Alexandra Cuffel, "Gendered Visions and Transformations of Women's Spirituality in Hayyim Vital's *Sefer ha-Hezyonot*," *Jewish Studies Quarterly*, Volume 18 (2011): 1–46.

enhanced our world and were embraced by us. Some women took it upon themselves to be educated, though perhaps not formally. They were not necessarily publicly acknowledged because the mainstream was not in accord with the general acceptability of their inclusion in leadership roles. Those of us who followed the mystical path knew that the women's contributions, the feminine spirit, and the wisdom the women offered were essential to realizing the full benefits of learning and unifying with the One. ***There is no balance without the energy of the feminine.*** There is a deficit without the feminine. Unification cannot occur without the inclusion of feminine energy.

Now, how this came about is a matter of interest. As with any group, there are those who contribute, those who are neutral, and those who diminish due to their reticence to participate in a positive manner. And some participate and contribute in less obvious, behind-the-scenes, yet positive and essential ways. The latter category mostly consisted of women in our day. The men did not, on the whole, deny themselves a place in the public forum and view. Some of the most powerful and potent resources were our women. Had this been known, it would have diminished our stature in the eyes of what was mainstream Judaism at the time. We cared more about authenticity and the desired result of our directed efforts, but a certain degree of acceptance was important to us and our cause. And so, the women appeared [to the outside world] to be silent. They were not, but their efforts were often couched as though they were our efforts. We were fed their insights and wisdom. We most often passed it on as though it had come directly from us.

Those women who imparted their talents and wisdom were indeed wise enough to know that if they did not disseminate it through us, the wisdom would not be spread as needed.

THE TRUTH OF SELF

May 15, 2020

All I have told you, all we have written together so far, has been toward this end. The details of my life and all my lives are many. The details carry our minds from one moment to the next, keeping us busy and distracted. But indeed, it is not the details that carry a life. What matters is how we carry ourselves from day to day, from stage to stage, through the challenges we are given and the ones with which we present to ourselves. The meaning of it all is the way we present ourselves, the way we deal with challenges, and how we carry ourselves.

The meaning of life is in how we manage the journey. It is not all the details, the endless details of letter permutation, meditative techniques, prayer ritual, religious restriction, alchemical formulations, etc. It is, in the end, all about facing our own inner destiny and our own individual challenges on the way to doing so. We can run in fear, hide in cowardice, layering upon ourselves the restrictive rules of society that do not apply to us, expectations of a family that keeps us in bondage, and anything else that keeps us from seeing, accepting, and living our Truth —

or, we can be courageous. We can be encouraged by the feelings that hold us in a loving embrace. These feelings let us know that we are home. [**That** is *Unification*], and we can refuse to accept the interference (whatever its form or origin) that keeps us from correctly reading and following our inner compass. The true Unification is with the Truth of the Self — for the Truth of the self is the Truth that we are already one with the One. We are of the One Source, separated by just a moment.

APPENDIX

SAFED AND RABBINIC BIOGRAPHIES

The small town of Safed (also spelled as Tzefat and Tzfat) flourished as a center of sixteenth-century Jewish ideals and spirituality in law, ethics, philosophy, and mysticism. Located in Northern Galilee and part of the Ottoman Empire, Safed connected common trade routes and became home to Jews from Spain (after the expulsion of 1492), Europe, Turkey, Egypt, and other areas.

The community that produced some of the influential Jewish works and ideas included Joseph Karo, Moses Cordovero, Moses Alshich, Isaac Luria, and Hayyim Vital, among others. Many others were students of these great men, as well as being known in their own right.

Moses Alshich (1508–1593) was born in Turkey and emigrated to Safed, where he became one of the era's great Torah scholars and commentators. He studied under Cordovero and later Luria. Hayyim Vital was one of his most renowned students. His standing in the world of Torah was such that he was known as Alshich HaKodesh (the Holy One). Hakadosh is a rare title and reflects the esteem Alshich held within his community and beyond. Although Alshich was a member of the circle of Kabbalists who lived in Safed, his works are not Kabbalistic but rather emphasize allegorical perspectives. Although not mentioned by R. Hayyim in this volume, he was the rabbi who gave *semikha*[89] to R. Hayyim in the 1590s.

Joseph Karo (1488–1575) was an eminent legalist whose codification of Jewish law, *Shulhan Arukh* (*The Set Table*), is authoritative to this day, as is his divinely inspired and channeled work, *Maggid Meisherim*. Some describe this maggid as an angelic presence, and some say that the maggid was the voice of the entirety of knowledge contained in the *Mishnah*. Karo was known in his day as *HaMechaber*, or "the Author."[90]

Moses Cordovero (1522–1570) was an exponent of the classical Kabbalah. A prolific writer, Cordovero, often referred to as the RaMaK, systematized a vast and disparate body of Kabbalistic lore. He was the author of *Pardes Rimonim* and the founder of the Cordoveran school. He developed the rationally influenced systemization of all Kabbalah that had been revealed up to that point in history. He was also the master teacher of Hayyim Vital prior to the arrival of Isaac Luria.

Isaac ben Solomon Luria Ashkenazi (1534–1572) was known as The Ari (HaAri — The Lion) and Arizal. Isaac's father died when he was eight, and so he and his mother moved from Jerusalem to his uncle's home in Egypt. HaAri's extraordinary learning capacity and his uncle's privileged position enabled him to study with the most learned men of Cairo. At the age of 21 he came upon a copy of the Zohar and secluded himself for six years on an island in the Nile to study the scroll. There, his teacher was

---

[89] *Semikha* is the traditional name for Rabbinic ordination. The practice had fallen away (mostly in Israel) in previous centuries and was experiencing a limited revival in the 1500s, so this was a major event at the time. Alshich himself received *semikha* from Joseph Karo.

[90] See "The Maggid of Joseph Karo" in the Appendix.

the spirit of the prophet Elijah. Elijah directed him to move to Safed at age 36 to become Hayyim Vital's teacher. Upon the death of the RaMaK, shortly after Luria arrived in Safed, he became the leader of the community and developed what became known as Lurianic Kabbalah. The Lurianic Kabbalah was based on HaAri's wisdom, knowledge, and insights added to the traditional teachings of the Zohar. His ability to read people and his incredible depth of knowledge about the mysteries of life created a cult-like following. Legends of his charisma continue to this day. He appointed his main disciple, Hayyim Vital, to record his teachings and wrote down virtually none of his own work. He died from the plague at the age of 38.

Although Luria wrote very little himself, his developments of the Kabbalah, primarily recorded by his chief disciple Hayyim Vital, shaped later Kabbalism and, ultimately, Hasidism, which was birthed in the eighteenth century. There is a limited amount of translated material from this time compared to the volumes written, but more has been translated in recent years. To quote Gershom Scholem, the twentieth-century scholar, "The Lurianic Kabbalah was the last religious movement in Judaism, the influence of which became preponderant among all sections of Jewish people and in every country of the Diaspora, without exception."[91]

---

[91] For a selection of his works, see "Rabbi Hayyim Vital" in the Appendix.

RABBI HAYYIM VITAL

Although there are conflicting details in the many accounts of Hayyim Vital's life, the following information is corroborated in many publications. There is much to learn about Hayyim Vital. This is a start.

Biography[92]

Rabbi Hayyim ben Yosef Vital Calabrese was born in 1543 in Safed into a family with origins in Calabria, Italy. R. Hayyim's father, Yosef, was a famed and skilled scribe who was highly respected for his work. Yosef's much sought-after *tefillin* (phylacteries) were said to have been written in holiness and purity with special Kabbalistic intentions.

R. Hayyim was renowned primarily as R. Yitzchak Luria's recorder and editor. However, he was also an accomplished Kabbalist and writer with a wide array of interests and areas of expertise in his own right. He was destined for greatness by all who knew him in his early years and was educated extensively at a very young age. Even at birth, he was considered a special child with many gifts. His father found Torah scholars and tutors to advance his levels and stages of Jewish learning. His destiny was confirmed at the age of 12 by a palm reader.

Young R. Hayyim was known for his aptitude and genius both in his own community and beyond. He studied Kabbalah under

---

[92] Adapted from Miller, "Rabbi Chaim Vital."

the leading Kabbalistic luminary in the world at the time, R. Moshe Cordovero (the RaMaK), and the revealed aspects of Torah under R. Moshe Alshich, one of the foremost rabbis of Safed. The great scholars and rabbis of the day invested their time and knowledge in R. Hayyim because they recognized his genius and expected much of him. The Maggid of Yosef Karo believed R. Hayyim was the successor of R. Karo. R. Hayyim was encouraged by his teachers, peers, and disciples to extract himself from all worldly matters and devote himself to the study of Kabbalah, which was promised as his path to greatness. This would significantly affect not only his academic and spiritual life but also his personal life.

At 23, R. Hayyim married his first wife, Hannah, the daughter of R. Moses Saadia, with whom he had a son and daughter. When R. Hayyim left his wife, the prophet Elijah appeared to him in an elaborate dream. The dream, or vision, convinced him that he was destined to become a Kabbalist. R. Hayyim devoted the following two and a half years to the study of alchemy, which, given the world he lived in, may have seemed to be an odd choice. Upon completing his studies, Elijah again appeared in a vision and told him that he would succeed in his academic efforts and write a commentary on the Zohar, which the RaMaK had taught as the primary text of Kabbalah.

In 1569, at age 26, R. Hayyim began writing his commentary on the Zohar. He was dedicated to this work until 1570, when Isaac Luria (HaAri) arrived in Safed from Egypt. A few months after his passing, the nature of his relationship with his former teacher, the RaMaK (and others), allowed R. Hayyim to call upon him in the Heavenly Academy. After spending a couple of years working on his commentary, the RaMaK appeared to R. Hayyim in a dream. The RaMaK told him to follow the way of HaAri and that his was the method taught in the Heavenly Academy.

R. Hayyim was not initially drawn to HaAri. Still, he became his chief disciple within a short period of time. R. Hayyim wrote of the depth of his connection and the intensity of his initiation into HaAri's new approach to Kabbalah.

'When I [first] came to my teacher of saintly memory [the Ari] to study this wisdom under him, he was about to leave for Tiberius. He took me with him. We boarded a boat, and as we were sailing [across the Kinneret] at a point opposite the arches of the Old Synagogue of Tiberius, my teacher dipped a cup into the water and gave it to me to drink. He told me that now I could grasp this wisdom [the teachings of Kabbalah], for I had just drunk water from the well of Miriam [which is buried in the Kinneret]. From that time on, I began to enter the depth of this.'[93]

R. Hayyim already had his own reputation as a stellar scholar, and his future was predicted as a lofty one, but within a year of his initiation into HaAri's teachings, he became a famous Kabbalist throughout Israel and the Diaspora. He was soon recognized as HaAri's successor.

HaAri was unaccustomed to writing down his teachings and designated only one person to record and pass them on — R. Hayyim. R. Hayyim details the reasons he was chosen in his *Book of Visions*. After HaAri's passing, he edited and organized their manuscripts. He also began teaching HaAri's Kabbalistic insights to his own disciples. He became the revered leader of an

---

[93] Miller, "Rabbi Hayyim Vital."

influential group of Kabbalists, although that had not been HaAri's intention. Members of this group signed an agreement that honored HaAri's wishes to keep his teachings in Palestine. Unfortunately, many of his disciples had already recorded the teachings against HaAri's explicit wishes.

In 1587, R. Moshe Alshich, R. Hayyim's teacher, appointed him as a leading judge in Jerusalem's rabbinical courts. He remained there for several years and then returned to Safed. In 1594, he moved to Damascus, where he passed away in 1620 at the age of 77.

Before he died, R. Hayyim ordered that all his manuscripts be buried with him. Several years later, after asking permission in a Kabbalistic rite, Abraham Azulai and R. Yaakov Tzemach, colleagues, and disciples of R. Hayyim, extracted the writings from his grave and published them. They claimed that the deceased author did indeed allow them to exhume the manuscripts. Some accounts say that this was done with his son Samuel's permission. Although many different editions of these works were published the century after his death, few were authentic.

Bibliography[94]

Shemoneh She'arim. Also known as *Etz HaChaim*, a collection that includes the following:

- *Shaar HaHakdamot* – on the emanation and creation of the worlds.

- *Shaar Mamarei Rashbi* – a commentary on some passages in Zohar.

- *Shaar Mamarei Razal* – a Kabbalistic explanation of various Talmudic dicta.

- *Shaar HaPesukim* – a commentary on the verses of Tanach.

- *Shaar HaKavanot* – divided into two parts. The first details matters pertaining to blessings and prayers; the second with matters pertaining to Shabbat and the Festivals (Venice 1624).

- *Shaar HaMitzvot* – a Kabbalistic explanation of the mitzvot.

- *Shaar Ruach HaKodesh* – meditations, Kabbalistic customs and *yichudim*-meditations.

- *Shaar HaGilgulim* - explains and describes the doctrine of transmigration and metempsychosis.

Shmoneh Shearim – Eight Gates

Sefer HaChizyonot – Spiritual Biography

---

[94] Adapted from Miller, "Rabbi Chaim Vital."

Other works:

- *Sefer HaKavanot* – mystical customs and meditations on the prayers.

- *Dodi Yarad l'Gano* – a poem printed in Shaarei Tzion (Amsterdam, 1671).

- *Sefer HaGilgulim* – explains and describes the doctrine of transmigration and metempsychosis (Frankfort on Maine 1684).

- *Nof Etz Chaim* (Frankfort on Maine 1684).

- *Likutei Torah u'Taamei HaMitzvot* – a Kabbalistic analysis of the mitzvot (Zolkove 1775).

- *Otzrot Chaim* – contains Kabbalistic doctrines similar in content to Etz Chaim (Koritz 1783).

- *Likutei Shas* – a Kabbalistic analysis of Talmudic statements (Livorno 1794).

THE MAGGID OF RABBI YOSEF KARO

R. Yosef Karo developed *Maggid Mesharim*, a written journal of transmissions from his Maggid. The Maggid was a spirit that made itself known to Karo through automatic writing[95] and channeled speech.[96] It is said that these transmissions came to him nightly and advised on all aspects of R. Josef's life. On Friday nights, several students would gather in Rabbi Karo's home to hear the Maggid's words as spoken by Karo himself.

Heavenly mentors were not altogether unusual with the Kabbalists in his circle; however, R. Karo was the most famous of those who were public with the information. The Maggid (roughly translated as the Preacher or Teller) was said to be his heavenly mentor. Over time, many believed that Maggid of R. Karo was the voice of the Mishnah, the compendium of Jewish knowledge and law[97] and present with the spirit of the Shekhinah.[98] Much of what

---

[95] Writing said to be produced by a spiritual, occult, or subconscious agency rather than by the conscious intention of the writer.
[96] When a person conveys thoughts or energy from a source believed to be outside the person's body or conscious mind, specifically one who speaks for nonphysical beings or spirits.
[97] "Compiled around 200 by Judah the Prince, the Mishnah, meaning 'repetition,' is the earliest authoritative body of Jewish oral law. It records the views of rabbinic sages known as the Tannaim (from the Aramaic 'tena,' meaning to teach)."
From Maimonides, "The First Complete Mishnah," *British Library Collection Items*, accessed January 16, 2023, https://www.bl.uk/collection-items/first-complete-mishnah.
[98] The feminine aspect of God.

is revealed in Karo's notes is material that informs the reader of intimate details of his life that could not be known any other way.

Yosef Karo compiled his mystical diary, which recorded the Maggid's revelations over roughly forty years. *Maggid Mesharim* was first published in Amsterdam in 1704.

SHABBATAI TZVI

The years of violence against European Jews in the sixteenth and seventeenth centuries gave birth to the great hope of a messiah who would rescue Jews from the depths of despair and destruction. It was as a result of such an environment that a false messiah appeared. In 1648, a man named Shabbatai Tzvi settled quietly in the Jewish community of Turkey and established himself as a learned scholar. As time passed, he connected his beliefs and practices more with the mystical. It is said he suffered from what we now call severe bipolar disorder,[99] which likely accounts for the extreme nature of many of his beliefs and activities. His perversion of Jewish rituals and norms was why he created a stir in whatever establishment he found himself in and was often cast out of the places he lived and visited.

Shabbatai Tzvi traveled to the Mediterranean countries, spreading his beliefs and practices to a minor degree until he encountered Nathan of Gaza around 1665. Nathan of Gaza believed himself a prophet possessed of mystical powers. It was through these powers that Nathan attributed a vision that Shabbatai Tzvi was indeed the messiah. Nathan promoted him to the world as such. With this new reputation, Shabbatai Tzvi began to attract more and more followers, and soon, there was a

---

[99] Matt Plen, "Who Was Shabbetai Zevi?" from *My Jewish Learning*, accessed November 18, 2022 from https://www.myjewishlearning.com/article/shabbetai-zevi/.

messianic fervor in the air. Although the rabbis disapproved of Shabbatai Tzvi, they took no action to excommunicate him.

The hopes that had arisen through the Kabbalah of Isaac Luria circa 1570 triggered Shabbatai Tzvi's initial acceptance by the people. Many Tzvi followers were ripe to being swept into a messianic tidal wave headed for redemption. The rabbis of the time somewhat heeded this aspiration so as not to lose their people. As the movement took on a life of its own, many of his followers followed him to the Holy Land and deeper into the Ottoman Empire.

Upon his 1666 arrest and imprisonment in Constantinople, the Sultan offered Shabbatai Tzvi a choice of death or conversion. Shabbatai Tzvi converted to Islam the next day, took a Muslim wife, and received a royal pension until he died in 1676. Although his actions sent his followers reeling, he secretly continued practicing his brand of Judaism and believing in his messianic mission. The movement was sustained for a while until it split into two. One movement was moderate, and the other radically rejected the Torah.

FOUR WHO ENTERED THE GARDEN

"Four Who Entered the Garden (Paradise)" has been the subject of myriad commentaries since the story first came into being in Talmudic times. The story illustrates many viewpoints and principles of spirituality, personality, and learning, all of which are explored in the commentaries. Even the words and actions in the simplistic version below illustrate principles, are open to many viewpoints, and convey great meaning.[100]

———◆———

The Talmud (Chagiga 14b, *Zohar I*, 26b, and *Tikunei Zohar*, Tikun 40) reports an incident regarding four sages from the time of the Mishnah (about 10 220 C.E.): Ben Azzai, Ben Zoma, Acher (Elisha Ben Avaya)[101] and Rabbi Akiva. These sages were said to be the greatest of their generation.

The rabbis taught that the sages entered Pardes (garden/Paradise/orchard) and ascended to Heaven using the Divine Name after intense meditation and prayer to elevate their spirits. Prior to their ascension, Rabbi Akiva gave them a warning: 'When you come to the place of pure marble stones, do not say,

---

[100] One of the foremost commentaries is by Rabbi Isaac Luria. See "4 Who Entered the Orchard," *Chabad.org: Kabbalah Online*, translated and edited by Moshe Yaakov Wisnefsky, accessed August 27, 2022,
https://www.chabad.org/kabbalah/article_cdo/aid/380400/jewish/4-Who-Entered-the-Orchard.htm.

[101] Acher means "the other." This name was given to him as a result of the very episode that happened in the garden.

'Water! Water!' for it is said, 'He who speaks untruths shall not stand before My eyes.' (Psalms 101:7)[102]

What happened to each of them on this journey was in accordance with their essence.

- Ben Azzai gazed (at the Divine Presence — Rashi) and died. "Precious in the eyes of G-d is the death of His pious ones." (Psalms 116:15)

- The verse regarding Ben Zoma states, "Did you find honey? Eat only as much as you need, lest you be overfilled and vomit it up." (Proverbs 25:16)

- Acher encountered plantings and cut them down. He became a heretic. (This is the reason he was given the name Acher.)

- Rabbi Akiva entered in peace and left in peace.

In other words, one looked and died, one looked and went mad; one looked and apostatized, and one entered in peace and departed in peace.[103]

---

[102] Luria, "4 Who Entered the Orchard."
[103] Elisha be Abuyah, *New World Encyclopedia*, accessed March 22, 2023 from https://www.newworldencyclopedia.org/entry/Elisha_ben_Abuyah.

THE KABBALISTIC TREE OF LIFE

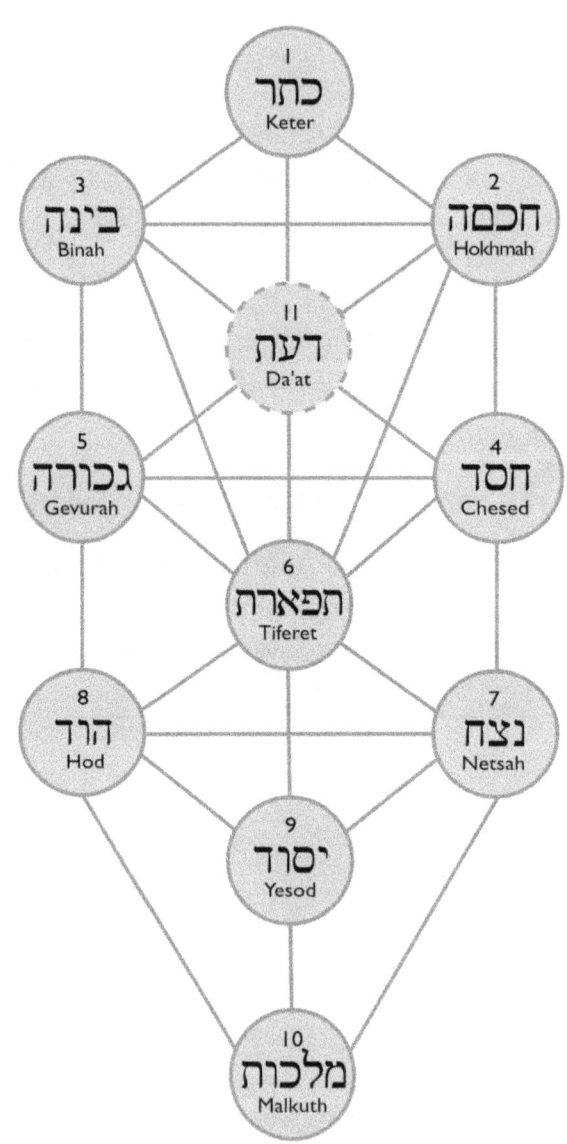

The ten sephirot of the Kabbalistic Tree of Life:

1. **Keter (Kether)** – *The Crown.* Represents super consciousness, the connection between the human and the divine.
2. **Hokhmah (Hokmah)** – *Wisdom.* Represents creativity, intuition, male energy.
3. **Binah** – *Understanding.* Represents stability, female energy.
4. **Chesed** – *Mercy, Kindness.* Represents benevolence, order, laws.
5. **Gevurah (Gevurah)** – *Power, Severity.* Represents strength, courage, righteousness.
6. **Tiferet (Tiphereth)** – *Heart, Beauty.* Represents individuality, coordination of parts, balance, symmetry.
7. **Netzach (Nezach)** – *Victory.* Represents emotion, art.
8. **Hod** – *Glory, Splendor.* Represents intellect, determination.
9. **Yesod** – *The Foundation.* Represents energy, imagination, communication.
10. **Malkuth** – *The Kingdom.* Represents the physical world and body, self-expression.
11. **Da'at** – Knowledge is not actually numbered and does not appear on most diagrams. Located in the center, just below Wisdom and Understanding.

ACKNOWLEDGMENTS

I want to first and foremost thank Hayyim Vital for having faith in me to deliver his message and for his very strong push to bring this book to publication. Believe me, it was not an easy task (getting me to finish, that is). He has also been my teacher in many ways outside of this book, and I thank him for that as well.

There is one amazing human who can never receive enough thanks from me. Without the sisterhood, friendship, and the mad skills of Janice Levie, I can honestly say that this book would never have seen the light of day. She came into my life fortuitously at a point where I was quite stuck and in need of an editor. She came into the project with incredible enthusiasm, intellectual curiosity, and massive editing skills. Jan was always kind and patient with me as we worked our way through a delicate process, growing a professional relationship and a valued friendship along the way. With any luck, she will stick with me through future projects. Thank you, Jan, for coming into my life and becoming my friend as well as my technical support and editor.

Thanks to Ismail Ogunbiyi for his kindness and patience with me and for his technical skill and support while transforming this manuscript into a book, and also to Cheakina for her beautiful and powerful book cover design.

I am blessed to have many friends who supported and encouraged the process of recording, researching, and editing this work. Each supported me in their own unique and loving way —

some with kind words and inquiries, some by reading entries as they were recorded, and some for reading the completed manuscript. Some simply listened for endless hours as I railed on about the fascinating and illuminating history I learned along the way. To all of you, I am most grateful.

Larry Artale, thank you for your indefatigable cheerleading and listening that helped me get to the finish line. Wanda Alexander, Sandra Cohen, Lisa Kimball, Terry Greenstein, Ellen Greenwood, and Farhanaz Ellis, thank you for your unending support and varying degrees of reading of R' Hayyim's words along the way. Invaluable. I thank the waiters (especially Maged and Mohamed) at the Sufi Café in Cairo for your sweet friendship, coffee supply, and for reserving my quiet table in the corner for months on end — even though you had no idea what I was up to.

With special gratitude, I would like to thank Jay Ledner for always shoring me up when I got frustrated or distracted, for sustaining my energy and spirit along the way, and for reading the drafts and final book manuscript. Jay, your comments and suggestions helped to sharpen my thoughts and understanding, which helped to shape the book and the clarity of the materials. You never declined the role of sounding board or friend and really kept me moving forward with your endless questions and energetic involvement. I consider your efforts to qualify you as a true collaborator in this effort and in my life. Thank you.

Helen Andrews, thank you for the friendship, encouragement, and patronage that brought this project to fruition and onto the printed page. May you find satisfaction and reward for all you have done.

For what you all have done, may you be blessed.

REFERENCES

"4 Who Entered the Orchard." *Chabad.org: Kabbalah Online*. Accessed August 27, 2022. https://www.chabad.org/kabbalah/article_cdo/aid/380400/jewish/4-Who-Entered-the-Orchard.htm.

"About Shulchan Arukh." *Sefaria*. Accessed January 20, 2023. https://www.sefaria.org/Shulchan_Arukh,_Even_HaEzer?tab=contents.

Arbel, Llil. "dybbuk." *Encyclopedia Mythica*. Accessed January 20, 2023. https://pantheon.org/articles/d/dybbuk.html.

"Authenticity of Maggid Mesharim." *Stack Exchange*. Accessed August 27, 2022. https://judaism.stackexchange.com/questions/56940/authenticity-of-maggid-mesharim.

ben Abuyah, Elisha. *New World Encyclopedia*. Accessed March 22, 2023. https://www.newworldencyclopedia.org/entry/Elisha_ben_Abuyah.

Brodt, Eliezer. "R. Chaim Vital and his Unknown Work Sefer ha-Pe'ulot: A Work on Science, Medicine, Alchemy and Practical Magic." July 8, 2010. Accessed October 20, 2022. https://www.academia.edu/37197602/R_Chaim_Vital_and_his_Unknown_Work_Sefer_ha_Peulot_pdf.

Cuffel, Alexandra. "Gendered Visions and Transformations of Women's Spirituality in Hayyim Vital's Sefer ha-Hezyonot." *Jewish Studies Quarterly*. Volume 18 (2011): 1–46.

Faierstein, Morris. "Grave Visitation by Rabbi Isaac Luria and Rabbi Menachem Mendel Schneerson." *Modern Judaism*. 36, no. 1 (2016): 31–41.

"The First Complete Mishnah." *British Library Collection Items*. Accessed January 16, 2023. https://www.bl.uk/collection-items/first-complete-mishnah.

Fischer, Laurie. "Parshat Behar: The Old Shall be Renewed and the New Made Holy." *Sefaria*. Accessed November 7, 2022. https://www.sefaria.org/sheets/234634?lang=bi.

Fishbane, Eitan P. "Perceptions of Greatness: Constructions of the Holy Man Shivhei ha-Ari." In *Kabbalah: Journal for the Study of Jewish Mystical Texts*, Volume 27 (Los Angeles 2012), 195–221. Accessed December 26, 2022. https://www.academia.edu/16574626/Perceptions_of_Greatness_Constructions_of_the_Holy_Man_in_Shiv%E1%B8%A5ei_ha_Ari.

Freedman, Harry. "Academy on High." *Jewish Virtual Library*. Accessed December 29, 2022. https://www.jewishvirtuallibrary.org/academy-on-high.

Freedman, Harry. "How to deal with a dybbuk." *The JC*. Accessed August 28, 2022. https://www.thejc.com/judaism/features/how-to-deal-with-a-dybbuk-1.479193.

Gottlieb, David. "Ana b'Koach: A Portal to Creation." *My Jewish Learning*. Accessed January 20, 2023. https://www.myjewishlearning.com/article/ana-bkoach-a-portal-to-creation/.

"The Healing Water from the Well of Miriam." *Temple of Miriam the Prophetess*. Accessed December 25, 2022. https://templeofmiriam.com.

JPS Hebrew-English TANAKH. Philadelphia: The Jewish Publication Society. January 1, 2001. Psalm 90:17.

Karpman, Joseph. "Klippah." *Atzmut*. Accessed January 18, 2023. https://atzmut.net/question/klippah/.

Maimonides. "The First Complete Mishnah." *British Library Collection Items*. Accessed January 16, 2023, https://www.bl.uk/collection-items/first-complete-mishnah.

Miller, Moshe. "The Holy Ari." *Chabad.org: Kabbalah Online*. Accessed August 28, 2022. https://www.chabad.org/kabbalah/article_cdo/aid/380758/jewish/The-Holy-Ari.htm.

Miller, Moshe. "Rabbi Chaim Vital." *Chabad.org: Kabbalah Online*. Accessed August 27, 2022. https://www.chabad.org/kabbalah/article_cdo/aid/380648/jewish/Rabbi-Chaim-Vital.htm.

Miller, Moshe. "Rabbi Yosef Caro's Works." *Chabad.org: Kabbalah Online*. Accessed August 28, 2022.

https://www.chabad.org/kabbalah/article_cdo/aid/380684/jewish/Rabbi-Yosef-Caros-Works.htm.

Plen, Matt. "Who Was Shabbetai?" *My Jewish Learning*. Accessed November 18, 2022. https://www.myjewishlearning.com/article/shabbetai-zevi/.

"Sabbatai Zevi." *Jewish American History.org*. Accessed January 2, 2023. https://www.jewishhistory.org/sabbatai-zevi/.

Scholem, Gershom. *Major Trends in Jewish Mysticism*. New York: Schocken Books, 1995.

Szarmach, Paul E., ed. "Jewish Mysticism in the Sixteenth Century." In *Medieval Mystics*, 129–202. Albany, New York: State University of New York Press, 1984.

Vital, Hayyim. *The Book of Visions*. In *The Classics of Western Spirituality, A Library of the Great Spiritual Masters*. Trans. Morris M. Faierstein. Mahwah: Paulist Press, 1999.

Vital, Hayyim. "Introduction." *Shaarei Kedusha (Gates of Holiness)*. Accessed October 10, 2022. Sefaia.org. https://www.sefaria.org/Shaarei_Kedusha%2C_Introduction?lang=bi.

Zaklikowski, Dovid. "The Chair of Elijah and Welcoming the Baby." *Chabad.org*. Accessed August 27, 2020. https://www.chabad.org/library/article_cdo/aid/144123/jewish/The-Chair-of-Elijah-and-Welcoming-the-Baby.htm.

ABOUT THE TRANSCRIBER

Rabbi Bonny Grosz is a long-time student of Kabbalah and mysticism who has studied with Rabbi Zalman Schacter Shalomi and other teachers of Jewish mysticism and metaphysics. Rabbi Grosz is a teacher, writer, spiritual counselor, channeler, energy healer, and traveler living in Virginia.

www.ingramcontent.com/pod-product-compliance
Lightning Source LLC
Chambersburg PA
CBHW021209100426
42735CB00045B/317